THE LESSONS
OF TEOTIHUACAN

"Most important, love doesn't die; it cannot die. It is not limited to the physical boundaries of time and space. To me, my wife—my soulmate—and I are living examples of that truth.

"But there's another lesson that's important. We're living on the earth and we must use worldly methods combined with our spiritual awareness for the greater good. The word *karma* means 'action.' When we stop questioning and speaking out against the things we feel strongly about, we give permission for our rights to be taken away. Indifference and apathy will bury us. . . ."

—Dick Sutphen

Psychic researcher, past-life therapist and seminar trainer Dick Sutphen is the author of over 400 self-help tapes and 12 metaphysical books, including the bestselling *Past Lives, Future Loves; Finding Your Answers Within; Predestined Love; You Were Born Again to Be Together* and *Unseen Influences* (all available from Pocket Books). Dick Sutphen has appeared on many major television shows, and performed the first nationally broadcast past-life regression on Tom Snyder's NBC "Tomorrow Show." Since 1977, almost 100,000 people have attended his world-famous seminars throughout the United States. Dick and his wife, Tara, live in Malibu, California.

Books by Dick Sutphen

Earthly Purpose
Finding Your Answers Within
Past Lives, Future Loves
Predestined Love
Unseen Influences
You Were Born Again to Be Together

Published by POCKET BOOKS

EARTHLY PURPOSE

DICK SUTPHEN

POCKET BOOKS

New York   London   Toronto   Sydney   Tokyo   Singapore

An *Original* Publication of POCKET BOOKS

POCKET BOOKS, a division of Simon & Schuster
1230 Avenue of the Americas, New York, NY 10020

To my Best Friend,
Lover and Soulmate,
My Wife,
Tara

Contents

Introduction

Knowledge of your past lives can help you to understand what *influences, restricts,* or *motivates* you in the present. My investigation of what happened in Teotihuacan 1400 years ago has helped me to understand my passions—to secure freedom, to battle repression, and to empower others to help themselves.

My past offers an explanation for my obsessive need to communicate metaphysical concepts. On a soul level I know the acceptance of these ideas would change the world. Can you imagine a civilization where people really accepted reincarnation and karma—accepted that every thought, word, and deed would have to be balanced, if not in this life, then in a future life? Karma means that you and you alone are responsible for absolutely everything that has ever happened to you—thus eliminating blame. With the acceptance of these basic precepts alone, we'd live in a world in which everyone accepted self-responsibility and practiced the golden rule. Idealistic? Of course, but every little bit of acceptance would help.

I teach these ideas, so have I accomplished the goal? No, but my growth continues. A very wise person once said, "He teaches best what he most needs to learn." In writing this book I realize how far I've come in fifteen years, and also how far I have to go to become the Master I idealize.

My zealousness for communications has helped me to fulfill the goal of a nationwide metaphysical network that communicates with millions of people a year via books, audio/video tapes, seminars, and *Master of Life* magazine. I've often been rightfully criticized as "commercial," which I define as being read or purchased by many as opposed to an esoteric few. How can you be successful uncommercially? I do, however, like to point out that volume does not necessarily reduce sincerity or lessen value.

A reviewer once said, "Sutphen's Zen/martial arts background is always apparent, and it doesn't work for a spiritual leader." Again, the critics are right. I abhor the idea of being a spiritual leader. Nobody needs a guru. Zen says it best: "There is nothing to seek and nothing to find. You're already enlightened, and all the words in the world won't give you what you already have. The wise seeker, therefore, is concerned with one thing only: to become aware of what he already is, of the True Self within."

On the other side of the coin are the Christian fundamentalists who have condemned me for years in their books and broadcasts. When they started to politically legislate the New Age out of existence in the mid-eighties, my wife Tara and I established a nonprofit organization to fight them. As a result, New Agers came down on us harder than the fundamentalists, claiming I was being militant, not metaphysical. I responded in print: "To bring about positive change, we must initiate positive action. When we stop questioning and speaking out against the things we feel strongly about, we give permission for our rights to be taken away. You can't change what you don't recognize, and too many good people don't recognize what is happening. That's why I'm speaking out. Those who would oppose everything identified with the New Age would like nothing better than for us to remain quiet, apathetic, and indifferent. Yes, let's use the metaphysical techniques of sending our antagonists light and love, but let's also share, alert, and network. We don't need to do this with malice or subversive tactics. It can be done very positively.

"Look at history and you'll find that indifference and apathy have never worked in response to oppression. Believing as you do, you may not be apathetic or indifferent, but ignoring the threat can produce the same result. Indifference is a militant thing that can destroy a nation and leave its citizens buried beneath the ruins."

Although I didn't know it at the time, much of that passion probably relates to what happened in A.D. 581–582 in Mexico. The same may be true of the rest of my communications, which are ultimately about *liberation*—freedom *of* the self and freedom *from* the self. Freedom of the self means literal freedom, and the freedom to become all you are capable of being in all areas of your life. Freedom from the self is an earthly purpose we all share. It is a matter of rising above fear and learning to express unconditional love. Fear includes all the fear-based emotions, such as anger, selfishness, jealousy, hate, repression, envy, greed, possessiveness, arrogance, egotism, malice, blame, resentment, insecurity, inhibitions, and guilt.

Some of this book is intensely personal and painful. The story includes some failures—"mistakes," as I prefer to call them. When someone in a seminar asks me about my "failed" marriages, I reply, "If you fell off a bicycle two or three times before you learned to ride it, you needed those mistakes to succeed. I don't advocate that you ignore faults or mistakes, but I suggest that you observe things as they are without labeling them as good or bad. Mistakes are part of learning. Don't judge them. Accept them and a quick correction can follow."

Because of my "mistakes," I've spent many years of my life investigating love and relationships. My most popular books are on this subject. *Earthly Purpose,* in addition to being an incredible reincarnation research project, is also a love story that begins eight years before I met Tara—my soulmate. In retrospect, I believe these were years of preparation—time for experiences that prepared us to appreciate each other when destiny finally manipulated circumstances to bring us together.

Earthly Purpose is both a story of mass reincarnation and my story. It begins when I am five years into a volatile marriage that included experimentation with the open-relationship ideas of the early seventies, and on-again, off-again separations. During the separations I often went to Mexico, seeking solace on the deserted beaches, where I wrote several poetry books. A notation at the bottom of the page in one of the books says, "By finding out what we don't want, we learn what we need."

I was a slow learner.

Dick Sutphen
Malibu, California

SECTION

I

"Get the Books Together"

CHAPTER ONE

Mexico

1974

Naked and shivering, waist deep in the Sea of Cortez, I sipped steaming black coffee and watched the July sun ascend from behind the mountain peak. Runners of light raced across the shadowed desert floor, through the palm trees, down the beach and into the water, bathing my body in welcome warmth.

Tracy combed her long blond hair, peering into the rearview mirror of the Land Rover, parked in the sand a few yards from the water. She was wearing a pink tank top and tight, faded Levi's, unbuttoned at the top. Our camp consisted of two sleeping bags, a propane stove, and a Coleman lantern hanging on a piece of driftwood. Beyond the beach, the blurred edges of a bomb-blasted building took shape as dawn illuminated the faded red crosses on the remaining walls of a World War II hospital. Wrong place, wrong time, wrong country. Like me.

"Hey, you seem pretty deep in thought," she said. "Still pining for your wife?"

"Just thinking about the *Catch 22* movie set over there. The idea of Mexico doubling for Europe."

"I'll bet Judy isn't pining for you, Richard."

I didn't answer.

"If you can't get her out of your mind, why did you drag me along with you to this backward country?" she asked.

"I didn't exactly drag you, Tracy."

"You didn't exactly discourage me, either."

"That doesn't mean I'm ready for a permanent relationship. Besides, what would your husband say? And what about the other guy, Frank, who's paying the rent on your apartment?"

"I think I should fly home," she said.

"If that's what you need to do," I said.

"I'll fix breakfast," she said.

Bob Seger's rock and roll filled the space between us in the Land Rover. I ran the deserted beach for a mile before finding a cutback to the road to San Carlos. Retired Americans living on Social Security and pension checks had created this Guaymas suburb built around sport fishing. Houses were cheap. Mexican maids cost a few pesos a day. The good life would last until the government decided to nationalize the housing.

I turned south onto Route 15 and stopped for gas in Guaymas. I handed the attendent nine dollars. He shook his head and held up three fingers. "Three more dollars? Bullshit!" I said. "That converts to nine bucks and you know it."

He shook his head in response, hit the side of the gas pump and shoved the three fingers at my face.

"Bullshit!" I shouted, slamming my fist on the top of the metal pump. "Stop ripping off the tourists and they might come back." At six-one, I towered over him, and my boots added another two inches. He backed off a few steps, gave me the finger, and walked slowly back into the gas station.

Tracy was laughing as I climbed behind the wheel. "In your hat, poncho, and three-day beard, you look

4

like Clint Eastwood intimidating the natives. All you need is a thin cigar."

I pulled back onto the highway, past the hero's monument, the native market, and the city pier. Deeper into Mexico. The four-wheel-drive Land Rover was almost new, and loaded with enough supplies for two weeks. Despite the Spartan interior and what was at best a rough and noisy ride, it got good mileage and had the off-road agility of a mountain goat.

"What you resist you draw to you," she said.

"I don't resist these people. I don't even dislike them," I replied. "But I can count on them to do stupid things. That's just what is."

"I love your spiritual way of handling conflict."

"Tracy, truth is what works! Buddha said that, or something like that. It's the game you play down here. This morning I won, two days ago the woman in the Hermosillo restaurant won." We had been grossly overcharged for breakfast. When I called them on it, the woman at the cash register began to scream. Scanning the patrons' scowling faces, I paid the check, but retrieved the table tip on my way out.

"Why haven't you ever learned the language?" Tracy asked. "You spend so much time down here."

"I can convert the money and translate most menus, find the local icehouse, buy Jack Daniel's or a cup of black coffee. It's enough."

She shook her head.

I continued, "It's their country. Their game. Graft is a way of life. They ask, 'Why don't more American tourists come to Mexico?' At the inspection station I paid the cop twenty dollars so he wouldn't take an hour to examine every item in the Rover. A professor was murdered above Guadalajara, and his new Bronco was found with a policeman at the wheel. A Texan was forced to pay officials thousands of dollars in fees and a bottle of Scotch in order to bring home the body of his son, killed in an accident. They plant roaches or seeds in American vehicles and planes to justify confiscation. All this makes for great gossip and lurid newspaper stories above the border. Gee . . . I don't know, asshole, why don't more American tourists come to Mexico?"

Three months earlier, about fifty miles out of San Luis on a lightly traveled road, five men in street clothes had stepped in front of my vehicle, waving their arms for me to stop. I'd often been stopped by the *federales,* but was going to run off the road and around them until I spotted a police car half hidden in the trees. The leader was a big, wild-eyed man who spoke broken English. "You running dope through our country," he said. It was a statement, not a question. They began searching the Land Rover, and the big guy found a gun in the glove compartment, a blank starter pistol. "Ha, ha!" he exclaimed gleefully, looking at me.

"It shoots blanks . . . a toy," I said, aware that possessing a gun in Mexico is a serious offense.

He nodded some more, pointed it at my head, smiled sadistically and slowly cocked the hammer. Not understanding English, his men froze, thinking the gun was real. "Ha, ha, ha," he laughed, and pulled the trigger. The shot exploded. There was stunned silence. Then he laughed some more. His men laughed. I didn't laugh. Thank God they hadn't yet found the .45 automatic I had built into a holster under my seat.

"I don't run dope. I don't even use dope. I write stories about your country," I said, pulling a copy of *Outdoor Arizona* out of the toolbox. Opening the magazine to my article, I handed it to him. The story, about survival techniques and camping on the forty miles of beach below El Golfo, was illustrated with a map of upper Mexico and a picture of me. He looked at it, glared at me, threw the magazine onto the passenger seat and shouted at his men in Spanish. They walked away to await another vehicle, driven by an American with less problem potential. Trembling, I proceeded on my way.

"I guess we're just immoral people in an amoral country," Tracy said, pulling me back to the present. "Where are we going today?"

"Does it matter?"

"You have a love/hate relationship with Mexico, with your wife, and with me. Maybe you're the problem."

She stopped talking and looked out at a plump woman walking slowly down the road, hunched beneath the weight of a basket of wet laundry that was balanced on her shoulder.

"I'd like to know where I stand," she said.

"You're looking for answers neither of us have," I said. "Even after months of this on-again, off-again separation, I haven't given up on my marriage. Intellectually, I know it's over, but emotionally I can't seem to let go. Right now, Judy's probably in Los Angeles with Mr. Up-and-Coming Country Singer. Here I am, hiding from myself in a third world country with the wife of a client. And she doesn't have any more clarity on her situation than I do on mine."

"I know I don't ever want to be with Jerry again," she said, her voice brimming with distaste.

"So, divorce him."

"I will."

"Frank's wondering where you are."

"So what? I'd rather be with you."

"You're with me."

"If you really wanted your marriage to work, you wouldn't be here with me . . . unless you're just trying to get even or make her jealous."

I thought about that, but said nothing.

"If our ages were closer, maybe we'd get along better."

"Maybe," I said.

She was twenty-six. I was thirty-seven. Her husband, Jerry, was an art director at a Phoenix, Arizona, advertising agency. I headed my own small creative-services studio in Scottsdale, and Jerry often commissioned us to handle advertising projects. The back half of my studio served as a thirty-five-seat "Hypnosis Center," where I explored metaphysical concepts with a group that met there Wednesday evenings. Tracy began attending the spring sessions, sometimes with Jerry. One time, as the first to volunteer for a past-life regression, she took me aside and whispered, "I'm having an affair. I won't talk about it in hypnosis, in front of my husband, will I?" She smiled like a naughty little girl and squeezed my hand.

Early in the warm Mexican afternoon, a few miles below Ciudad Obregón, the sky clouded over and drops of rain began to splatter on the windshield. If it rained heavily, we'd have to find a hotel for the night. In an emergency we could sleep on a plywood shelf in the back of the Rover, but it was so cramped I couldn't even turn over without jamming my shoulder between the bedroll and the metal roof. Obviously, this eliminated the potential for any sex, so we either camped out or stayed in hotels. What the two of us lacked in compassion we made up for in lust.

At Navojoa, a sign pointing into the mountains said ALAMOS. The kilometers converted to thirty-two miles. My map indicated it was a dead end, the road in being the only way out. "Let's check it out," I said.

"Why?"

"I'd just like to."

Tracy shrugged her shoulders without replying,

picked up the *Mexico Guide* and began thumbing through the pages.

Turning left off the main highway, the narrow road began to ascend. The higher we went, the harder it rained. "Alamos," she said. "Want to hear about it?" She began reading without waiting for a reply. "'A Jesuit mission was established here in 1630, but the town grew in 1684 as the result of silver mining. Of its past grandeur, there remain only the arcades of what were once colonial mansions and the cobblestone streets. Originally named "Real de la Limpia Concepcion de los Alamos," and also "Real de los Frailes," it became Alamos in 1831 when the states of Sonora and Sinaloa were separated. The facade of the parochial church retains the richness of the colonial period, and the entire town offers the tranquillity and atmosphere of the Mexican province.

"'The town is built around Guadalupe Hill, with the Alamos mountains to the south and the big Chihuahua Sierra Madres range to the east. The king of Spain sent his Surveyor General to lay out the streets of Alamos in 1750. Beautiful patios are hidden behind walls, and early Spanish colonial-style windows have a *reja*, or balcony with decorative metal bars, that were needed for protection in the early days.'

"The street map looks like it's pretty small," she continued, "but they seem to have all the conveniences. A jail, city hall, post office, bus station, and an 'old tequila distillery.'"

At the edge of town we came to the high-walled patios, and I maneuvered very slowly through the narrow, rain-slick street. An occasional open door provided a brief glimpse of tiled outdoor floors, fountains, and colorful flowers. A few sad-eyed children stood under wide archways, waiting for the rain to stop. After several blocks the street opened into a beautiful plaza, with a bandshell and benches, that served as the town square. It was edged on all four sides with some of the tallest palm trees I'd ever seen. Colonial-style arched buildings were on two sides of the square, and a magnificent church covered the whole block at the far end. I pulled the Rover to the curb in front of the Hotel Los Portales, looked at Tracy, then nodded at the hotel. "Let's splurge."

She smiled. "Let's."

I ascended the long steps to the entrance and stepped through double doors into unexpected elegance. A man in a tuxedo stood at attention by the entrance to a glass-walled, atrium-style restaurant. On each table was a fresh red rose in a crystal vase, neatly centered on the white tablecloth. Although it was dinnertime, the restaurant was empty.

As I walked across the gleaming hardwood floor, my rain-soaked boots squeaked and oozed water from the holes in the sides. My poncho was dripping, and the tuxedoed clerk almost winced when I took the saddle bags off my shoulder and laid them on the counter. Nevertheless, he quickly recovered his composure and said, in perfect English, "Good evening, sir, may I help you?"

I filled out the registration card he gave me, but water trickled onto it from the brim of my straw Stetson and the ink ran, so I had to ask for another one. I looked down at the wet floor, noticed the hole in the right knee of my faded Levi's, and then glanced over at the maitre d'. He's not reading me as a big tipper, I thought.

After a shower and change of clothes, we sat on the second-story porch of Los Portales, overlooking the Plaza de las Armas. We ordered drinks: tequila and tonic for Tracy, a shot of Jack Daniel's in a cup of black coffee for me. We drank without talking, watching the rain and an occasional figure scurry across the square. I was fascinated by such a large Catholic church in such a small town. The town must have been bigger during the heyday of the mines.

"The guidebook says the church was built on the site of the original Jesuit mission," Tracy said. A shiver ran up my arms.

I knew that if I were to walk across the street and through those doors, I would see gold and silver treasures lining the walls of the sanctuary. And if I were to walk a couple of blocks in any direction, I would see the poverty of the parishioners, living in tiny one-room adobe houses with dirt floors, entire families subsisting on a diet of beans and tortillas. "Fuck the Catholic church," I said.

"Huh?" Tracy asked.

During summer, dusk lingers late in the hills that slope down toward Mexico's Pacific coast. Back in our room we made love for a long time. The rain was letting up. We read. I reviewed some of my journal writings:

> Karma dance
> karma
> dance
> now I can see
> I did it to you
> and
> you do it to me
> Karma dance
> karma
> dance
> look deeper
> and see
> you do it to you
> and
> I do it to me.

• • •

Words of unending love
chronicled on the back
of photographs
the flyleaves of books
and the cards and
letters of my life

empty words

meaningless words
briefly felt and
quickly forgotten

ghost words that echo
sarcastically across
years of cold reality

• • •

Just when I think
the anger is gone
an iridescent
bluish-red appears

A cold red that's
lost its fire and
lives in shadows
of icy calculation

Just when I think
the anger is gone
it's sunset in December
in Deadhorse, Alaska

Lying on the bed, I stared at the designs in the pressed-tin ceiling. It was painted vivid aquamarine. "Everything in Mexico is painted white, aquamarine, or coral," I said. Tracy agreed. I tried to write and gave up. I couldn't relax. When I closed my eyes, anxiety seemed to well up from the depths of my soul.

"It's stopped raining. I think I want to go for a walk," I announced, starting for the door.

"Can you wait half a minute for me to get my shoes on so I can go with you?"

Outside, the church pulled at me. We walked across the square and up the stairs toward the beckoning open doors. The interior was ablaze with light, and I could see the rows of votive candles, their flames flickering in the cool air. A few native women, kerchiefs on their heads, were coming, going, praying. The church walls were adorned with the expected treasures. "Let's go in," Tracy said.

"Never," I replied, setting off down the stairs and into the twilight, Tracy racing to keep up. I walked at a brisk pace, scarcely paying attention to where I was going except to head away from the plaza. I turned right down Zaragoza, a street of darkened doors and windows. As we got farther away from the plaza, the paved streets turned to hardened mud. A bent old man with a pushcart offered to sell us something, but I didn't acknowledge him. We cut down a back alley and were soon in the poorest section of town. A vacant-eyed woman swept the dirt in front of her house while a naked child clung tightly to her sack dress, sucking his thumb.

"Please slow down," Tracy pleaded. "What's the hurry?"

I was sweating profusely. Probably the humidity, I thought. I heard a man say, "Go home, gringos," but I saw no one. Then we were past the houses, out of town and across the Arroyo Agua Escondida, walking up the dirt road to a walled cemetery. The moment I saw it, I stopped. Long seconds passed as I hesitated; then I walked on. Reaching the wall, I touched it gently, tears welling up in my eyes. I shook my head in confusion and moved forward, following the wall, looking for the entrance. Faster. Tracy fell behind. Inside, I increased my pace as I strode between the markers and the monuments and the crypts. The world was spinning. It was getting dark. I stopped and sank to my knees, both fists clenched tightly to my chest. I was sobbing like a hurt child.

CHAPTER TWO

Mexico
1974

San Blas is tropical, its steamy jungle much as I imagine the South Seas to be. Wild parrots bask in the heat, flitting from tree to tree and squawking so loudly you can't carry on a conversation in the town plaza. The church is the only building of importance. Route 46 runs into town from the highlands, past the plaza, the shacks, and small adobe buildings, ending at the native fishing docks at the mouth of a lagoon. If you turn left off 46, onto cobblestone-paved Calle Lanzagorta Sur, you end up at the Pacific Ocean.

For three days we camped at Los Cocos Beach, living on fresh channel bass purchased from a Los Angeles hippie who was fishing the estuaries. He told me about a backyard tortilla maker and suggested I buy a banana knife at the general store. I did. The three-foot-long knife was made of cheap steel, with a double-edged blade that widened in the middle, then tapered toward the rounded tip. In the nearby jungle I cut down more bananas than we could eat in a month.

The more I tried to forget the incident in the Alamos cemetery, the more vividly I remembered it. It was the first time I had cried in years. And for no reason.

We left San Blas and drove through Guadalajara, stopping only for gas. I love the Mexican back country and small towns, and I've found that the big cities are always trouble.

"How far down are we going?" Tracy asked when we arrived in Taxco. On a map of the world, Taxco was well below the Tropic of Cancer, aligned longitudinally with the Sudan in central Africa. "You know, you aren't going to find anyplace where you can hide from yourself," she said.

I didn't respond. Taxco, a town filled with quaint old colonial architecture, nestled in the mountains and populated by 23,000 people, is possibly the most picturesque place in Mexico. I liked it here. Sea-level dwellers, Tracy and I quickly became winded as we explored the steep streets of the mile-high town. Real de Taxco was founded by Cortez to exploit the silver mines in the area, and it remained a bustling boomtown until the 1800s, when the mines finally played out and it reverted to a sleepy village. In modern times a university professor decided to market Taxco's history by training young silversmiths and opening silver shops for the tourists. Today, the Mexican government has designated Taxco a national monument.

In the open-air native market below the plaza, vendors sold jewelry, ponchos, embroidered clothing, and food. We watched as an assertive young taco seller stripped the meat from the prominently displayed skull of what appeared to be a goat. "I think he wants people to know it isn't cat meat," I said. Then we found a place to sit down, next to two plump Indian women who let us share their picnic table.

"Let's start back north," I suggested as we ate lunch. The wind was whipping the white canvas tarps of the vendors' stands around so loudly it was difficult to talk. "I hate to go near Mexico City, but I feel drawn to Teotihuacan."

On our way to Mexico City we stopped at the Xochicalco archeological zone near Cuernavaca. The few Mexicans who lived at the edge of the site appeared to survive by selling warm soda pop to the tourists. The only flavor was orange. Their subpoverty-level shacks stood only a hundred yards from the ruins of a once great ninth century civilization. It bothered me.

Looking down from the top of a structure called the "higher monument," I saw the remains of a world that could have rivaled the beauty of any ancient center of civilization. Only a few of the main structures and a ball court had been uncovered and restored, but beyond them were endless mounds hiding the temples and centers of commerce that had once gleamed in the mountain sunshine. Thousands had worshiped and traded here, and had looked upon these same bas-relief carvings of Quetzalcoatl, the great plumed serpent.

Standing in the I-shaped ball court with its sloping sides, I tried to imagine the ritual-like game . . . the players wearing heavy padding on their bodies and helmets with eye slits as protection from the hard rubber ball that traveled at bone-shattering speed . . . the two rival teams vying for possession of the ball and attempting to knock it through a raised vertical stone hoop. As in soccer, the players could not use their hands, so scoring was difficult. It is said that winners earned glory and riches, but losers were sometimes killed. The two teams represented rival political factions, and the outcome of a game might determine weighty matters of state. Similar ball courts are to be found all over Mesoamerica.

My guidebook claimed that Xochicalco was a sacred city and fortress, presumably part of the Toltec culture, and a center of worship after the fall of Tula and Teotihuacan. This was true, unless it wasn't. I mistrusted the Mexicans' lax acceptance of their history. A Xochicalco codex, carved in stone, had been recovered and was owned by the village of Tetlama, but had yet to be studied. I could imagine it being used as the mayor's coffee table.

While Tracy was examining the relief carvings of priests with huge headdresses that lined both sides of the steps leading to a large ceremonial platform, I walked away, past the restored buildings, past the mounds, and into the growth of scrub desert and trees. Everywhere were the footings of houses or apartments. Square carved rocks formed a wall here, a half wall there. Trees grew in the middle of rooms where families had lived. Kids once ran up and down these narrow streets. Women ground the corn to make tortillas. Men came home after days of labor to eat meals and make love to their wives. These were people concerned about the same things that concerned me: relationships, children, daily work, the next meal.

"I walked at least a mile, and the ruins just go on and on," I said to Tracy, who was sitting on the steps of a ceremonial platform that might have been used for human sacrifice. The Toltecs were big on cutting out human hearts.

"I wish you'd told me where the hell you were going," she said.

"Many caves and passages under here," said a white-bearded, wrinkled old man who had walked up behind us. He was stooped and carried a modern Coleman lantern. "For five dollars I show you Los Amates."

I quickly agreed, and we followed the man down a steep, winding path in the hillside that ended at the mouth of a cave. The wind extinguished several matches before he was able to light the lantern. Inside, the Coleman tossed eerie shadows on the walls of the passageway, which opened into a large ceremonial room. There were smoke stains on the ceiling near a small hole that looked out on blue sky. Traces of paint could still be seen on the walls. "Was once covered with brilliant colors and pictures," said the old man, with a sweeping motion of his hand.

We arrived in Mexico City late at night, a mistake since the street names changed every few miles and my map bore little resemblance to reality. I decided to stop and look for another map in the back of the Land Rover, but while I was trying to find it, a jar of strawberry preserves fell from a shelf onto my sleeping bag. I watched as the lid rolled one way and the jar the other, spewing red jam across the yellow Indian design.

Tracy laughed apologetically. "My parents always called me 'lids off' because I couldn't remember to make sure the tops were on tight."

Suddenly, I exploded, verbally releasing all my frustrations with her and my anger at being lost in the world's largest city.

"What is, is," she responded calmly. "I'm a person who doesn't tighten jar tops. You'll just have to remember to pick them up by the bottoms."

That was the end of our conversation. Near dawn we arrived at the archeological zone of Teotihuacan (pronounced "Teh-oh-tee-wah-kahn"), thirty miles northeast of Mexico City. Parking in a wooded area nearby, we slept on the shelf in the back and were awakened in the morning by a herd of bleating sheep bumping against the Rover and rocking it back and forth. I looked out the slit of a window and saw a Mexican cowboy on horseback slapping a coiled rope against his leg to encourage the sheep to hurry along.

In addition to being sweaty and dirty, we now had

come down with "Montezuma's revenge." Our short tempers grew even shorter. Breakfast consisted of cold tortillas and Coleman-stove instant coffee. Sitting on the front fender of the Land Rover, sipping my coffee, I could see the top of the Pyramid of the Moon in the distance. The sight made me shiver.

They charged two pesos to let us park at the main entrance, and three pesos each to enter the archeological site. I purchased a cup of much better coffee from a vendor, and felt nearly human by the time we walked out onto the Street of the Dead.

The majesty of the partially restored city was awe-inspiring. Although only the bare bones of the former metropolis remained, I could almost imagine what it must have looked like when all the structures were standing, each covered with a smooth, gleaming lime plaster, painted in bright colors and adorned with murals. Teotihuacan was far more vast than its contemporary, Imperial Rome, covering more than twelve square miles and housing at its height over 200,000 inhabitants, organized into an elaborately stratified society. The city was a religious, cultural, economic, and political capital, as well as the greatest known market center in Mesoamerica, and home to a highly evolved people participating in a great master plan. But unlike the City of the Caesars, Teotihuacan was dedicated to the arts of peace rather than war. The beautiful, formal sculptures and wall paintings are said to have been the equals of those created in Renaissance Italy.

The paintings themselves reveal an intensely religious people, and the city was the seat of a religion with wide appeal, possibly headed by a supreme pontiff. Other archeological evidence suggests there may have been as many as four corulers, but there is little doubt that the city was governed by a theocracy—a form of government in which God or a deity is recognized as the supreme civil ruler, or a system of priests claiming a divine commission. Conventional archeologists, however, are unable to tell us anything more about the rulers who guided Teotihuacan's destiny, for their names and deeds are unrecorded.

In 1971 a tunnel was found running through the bedrock beneath the Pyramid of the Sun and ending in a series of chambers; the shape resembled a four-leaf clover. They were divided by man-made walls. Gouged in the floor were fire pits and water channels. Archeologists believe the tunnel suggests the existence of some kind of cult, which used these chambers as its inner sanctuary.

Archeologist Rene Millon's 1962 aerial photographs revealed more than 2200 apartment compounds in addition to the city's temples, platforms, and other major structures. Researchers agreed that most of the inhabitants lived by cultivating the land outside the city, but a significant number were crafts people, primarily obsidian workers who manned some five hundred local workshops. (Obsidian, a glassy volcanic rock, is similar in composition to granite, usually dark, but transparent when cut into thin pieces.) There was also evidence of over a hundred other kinds of workshops, which produced figurines, ceramics, cut stones, and ground stones as well as basalt, slate, and shale.

Carbon dating and historical research indicate that the city was founded about 200 B.C. and survived a thousand years. The population peaked between A.D. 450 and A.D. 650, and the city reached the apex of its power and influence around A.D. 500, when it appears to have enjoyed a Golden Age of peace and prosperity. By sometime in the 600s, however, the culture had begun to decline and degeneration had set in; warriors and military figures do not appear in paintings until the latter period. In the eighth century A.D., Teotihuacan suffered a major disaster, which ended in total collapse. Archeological and other evidence proves that at that time the city was sacked, burned, and partially destroyed.

"Kind of takes your breath away, doesn't it?" Tracy asked.

Facing north, over half a mile away on the right side of an ancient thoroughfare, the Pyramid of the Sun dominated the skyline, with its five tiers forming truncated cones that ended in a flattened top where the temple of the god had stood. The entire structure covered eleven acres and was as large as the great Pyramid of Cheops in Egypt, though not as tall. At the end of the main street stood the slightly smaller Pyramid of the Moon.

"Let's walk down to the Pyramid of the Moon and then work our way back to here," I suggested. Tracy nodded her approval, and we headed north, across the bridge spanning the San Juan River, drawn by the sheer grandeur of what once was.

At the top of the Pyramid of the Moon I looked out over the Valley of Mexico. To the south a cluster of snowcapped mountains soared like guardian gods 18,000 feet into the azure sky. And before them lay the green valley, then, as now, the center of civilization for all of Mexico. Within the archeological site in front of me reposed the great plaza and solemn rows of temple platforms. When the Aztecs arrived hundreds of years after the fall of Teotihuacan, they named the boulevard the "Street of the Dead," for they believed the ruins were the work of giants. The street runs 15° 30' east of north, and is said to align with the position of the setting Pleiades at the time of its construction.

The first phase of the city's history is believed to cover the two centuries before A.D. 0, but as early as

200 B.C. the valley was already an extended village of thousands. By A.D. 0, 40,000 to 50,000 inhabitants had pushed the far northwestern edge of the city as far as it would ever reach. No one knows what ignited the expansion, but these people began to build on a colossal scale. While most Mesoamerican cities grew haphazardly, Teotihuacan was laid out by master planners in a rectangular gridwork of streets and apartment blocks. This period witnessed the construction of the massive Pyramid of the Sun, twenty-three temple complexes—each formed by three temples built around a closed patio—and hundreds of apartment compounds and other buildings.

The second phase extended from A.D. 0 to A.D. 350, when Teotihuacan grew from a city-state into a metropolis. The Pyramid of the Moon and the Temple of Quetzalcoatl were major structural additions, and monumental sculpture and architectural refinements were introduced as well.

From A.D. 350 to A.D. 650, Teotihuacan reached the pinnacle of its power and glory. Monuments were built on a giant scale, the Temple of Quetzalcoatl was covered over with a larger building, and new structures were put up close to the Pyramid of the Moon.

People, many carrying cameras, were beginning to fill the Street of the Dead by the time Tracy and I began to explore the Palace of the Quetzal Butterfly. It was located behind a large platform on the west side of the Plaza of the Moon. We entered through a patio formed by twelve quadrangular pillars, each carved with fantastic creatures, part bird and part butterfly.

Most of the excavated wall surfaces were adorned with painted murals. Forty structures have been uncovered thus far, and even though only their lower walls remain standing, they have revealed a total of 350 murals. Teotihuacan was clearly a beautifully painted city, and much of its art relates to the culture's religious beliefs. Murals found not only on the walls of temples, but in the apartment compounds of ordinary citizens, display pictures of bird serpents, double-headed jaguars, feathered jaguar serpents, ordinary citizens, priests, and a number of symbols— fifty-seven signs that have been identified as writing glyphs. Yale art historian George Kubler suggests that the frontal figures in the paintings are cult images, while those shown in profile are human.

The Pyramid of the Sun was once painted bright red and polished to a glossy sheen. Standing at the top, I looked out at the earthen mounds yet to be excavated, each hiding a piece of history. "Can you imagine, some day hundreds of years in the future, people climbing to the top of the ARCO Tower in Los Angeles and looking out over the remains of a once great civilization?" I said.

In the huge courtyard of the citadel were raised platforms. Landing platforms, I thought. Then I wondered why I thought so. I had never had the slightest interest in UFOs.

Tracy played photographer while I attempted to mentally assimilate this lost world. It was starting to get to me—I couldn't touch it, I didn't understand it, and it seemed ominous, as if a dark undercurrent of energy were permeating the environment. We explored the remaining structures, but by late afternoon I wanted to leave; maybe wanted to get away would be more accurate.

After driving until we were exhausted, we found a luxurious country hotel called La Mansion. It was modern Mexico at its finest. Hand-carved furniture filled the cozy room. Reproductions of pre-Columbian sculpture sat on the dresser and nightstands. Bright, colorful Mayan and Toltec designs were repeated throughout the room on the bedspread, the curtains, and the loomed rugs that covered the uneven terra-cotta-tiled floor.

After cleaning up, we enjoyed a swim in the pool and a quiet dinner in the hotel restaurant. But on the way back to our room I started shaking and fell into a cold sweat. Lying on the hotel bed, I closed my eyes and was back in the ancient city, but there were no ruins. Instead, a magnificent complex of buildings, alive with thousands of people, gleamed whitely in the torchlit darkness. Fire leaped into the black sky from atop the Pyramid of the Moon, and elegantly robed men lined the steps from top to bottom.

"What's wrong? What's happening to you?" Tracy asked, trying to calm my thrashing and moaning.

"They're all here, all of them . . . I'm in the center of the ring at the base," I answered in an agitated tone of voice. "Everyone is looking at me. He's talking to me . . . I don't understand. I don't even know what you're talking about! I don't know about any books— I'm supposed to get the books together, and I haven't done it. The man standing halfway up the pyramid keeps telling me. It's as if I were on trial . . . they're all expecting me to get the books together."

Awakening from the comalike trance, I found the exhaustion was gone. "Good God, what in the world was that all about?" Tracy said.

"I don't know. I feel like a child who's just been reprimanded. That has to be the most vivid vision I've ever had. I'm supposed to find the books. It's my assignment, and I guess I've blown it. I don't have the faintest idea what the hell they were talking about. Probably something happened in a past life, and our visit caused subconscious memories to surface." But even as I said it, I knew it didn't fit. The "me" of today was somehow being chastised from beyond time by those who had once lived in Teotihuacan.

I sat on the edge of the bed, my eyes wide open. When I closed my eyes, vague outlines of the images slowly surfaced again. There was the Pyramid of the Moon, and thousands of people on the Street of the Dead. Soon those impressions faded, to be replaced by the Pyramid of the Sun. I was on top of the pyramid, dressed in a white tunic, holding a crystal rod as a barrier between myself and the masses of people attempting to scale the structure. The rod glowed and pulsated blue, somehow holding them back. "Back! Back! Back!" Shaking my head violently, I grasped for the present. "Teotihuacan." The words of the government guide surged through my mind. "Teotihuacan means 'the place where men became gods!'"

Unsteadily, I got up and walked out onto the balcony. "The sky is blacker in Mexico," I had once written in a poem. It was still true. Two stories below, reflected lights danced on the water as a lone swimmer gracefully stroked across the turquoise pool. The soothing rustle of palm leaves in the summer breeze made me feel at home, and the distant sounds of mariachi music weren't loud enough to intrude. The world's worst music and the world's best food, I thought for the thousandth time.

As I sat in the blackness of the hotel balcony, a strange poem I had written in my journal came to mind:

> He emerged from the
> shadows of the
> past as a dimly
> remembered dream
>
> naked
>
> betrayed

repeating your name

   bleeding in the
   tracks you
   left as you ran

   remember

   remember

He sent me ahead
to tell you
to remember.

Two days later Tracy decided to fly back to Phoenix, pick up her car, and return to her parents' home in Portland, Oregon. We said good-bye in the Durango airport. A sense of relief flooded through me as her plane lifted off the runway. Back in the Land Rover I headed to the coast, to Mazatlán, and then north to San Carlos and a deserted beach.

Alone in the sun, I read the many books on Teotihuacan I had purchased along the route. No one knows who built the metropolis. In the city's final years the Toltecs used it as a religious center, but even at its zenith it was inhabited by many other peoples— Mayans, Zapotecs, and others whose names are lost to history.

According to Sister Mary Corde Loraang in her book, *Footloose Scientist In Mayan America,* the five-thousand-square-foot top tier of the Pyramid of the Sun was once crowned not only with a temple structure, but also with a great idol of Tonacatecuhtli, the "Giver of Life." It was six feet wide, six feet thick, eighteen feet high, and carved from a single block of porphyry.

One passage from another book particularly affected me. Sixteenth century chronicler Fray

Bernardino de Sahagun, in Book Ten of his *History,* tells a story that can be linked to the fall of Teotihuacan, the first event in Mexican history referred to in any written source. He says nothing of why the city fell, but describes the departures of the "wise men."

. . . The wise men remained not long; soon they went. Once again, they embarked and carried off the writings, the books, the paintings; they carried away all the crafts, the castings of metals. And when they departed, they summoned all those they left behind. They said to them: "Our lord, the protector of all, the wind, the night, saith you shall remain. We go leaving you here. Our lord goeth bequesting you this land; it is your merit, your lot. Our lord, the master of all, goeth still farther, and we go with him. Whither the lord, the night [and] the wind, our lord, the master of all, goeth, we go accompanying him. He goeth, he goeth back, but he will come, he will come to do his duty, he will come to acknowledge you. When the world is become oppressed, when it is the end of the world, at the time of its ending, he will come to bring it to an end. But [until then] you shall dwell here; you shall stand guard here . . .

CHAPTER THREE

Arizona
1975–82

My wife Judith moved to Sedona, Arizona, and then to Darby, Montana, to live with a silversmith. A divorce soon followed. Tracy returned to Scottsdale. We dated and ended up living together.

In 1975 I bought a small redwood house on an old gold claim in Groom Creek, a mountain community above Prescott, Arizona. I wanted to write metaphysical books, and figured I could maintain enough freelance corporate advertising clients to survive in the solitude of the mountains.

Phoenix was 120 miles south; twice a week I made a run to the valley to collect assignments from advertising agency friends. Texaco Oil, in New York City, was one of my clients; when they called, I flew into the Big Apple wearing my Stetson, poncho, Levi's and boots, with saddle bags slung over my shoulder. Looking back, I'm surprised the Texaco executives were able to see through my attire but we worked successfully together.

In Prescott I met David Paladin, a Navajo/Anglo artist who signed his work with his tribal name, "Chethlahe." His paintings hung in galleries major collections throughout the world. A teacher of parapsychology at free-thinking Prescott College, Paladin also verbally channeled several discarnate entities, including Wassily Kandinsky, the famous Russian abstract painter who had died in 1944.

In September 1975, David and his wife Lynda came to our house for dinner. Following the meal, our conversation turned to the subject of Mexico, for I found David's affinity for the country paralleled my own. We were soon exchanging stories of our experiences below the border.

"What about Alamos, Sonora, David?" I said. "It has to be one of the most beautiful towns in all Mexico."

David said, "I agree with you, but I had an experience there that took me a while to get over. The cemetery on the edge of town, are you familiar with it?"

Goose bumps ran up and down my arms. "Oh, yes."

"Well, I completely broke down there," he said. "I went to pieces, and they had to literally carry me out of the place. They took me to the local seeress, who worked for a while at calming me down. I explained to her that I'd seen an old white church on the site." He paused and looked directly at me. "There is no such structure there now."

I clenched my fingers so tightly that I cut off the circulation. David continued.

"The seeress explained the situation to me, and said that during the Spanish conquest there was such a structure on the site. As the Spanish moved north through Mexico, they tried to convert the Indians to Christianity, but in what is now Alamos, they found a [...] resisted all their efforts. Finally the Spanish [...] to use force. They castrated the men, cut [...] and poked out their eyes, but to no [...] murdered five hundred natives and buried them in a mass grave. Immediately following the executions, Spanish soldiers began dying for no obvious reason. 'Dropping like flies,' she said. They placed the Christian graveyard on top of the Indian burial site as a form of exorcism, to quiet the evil spirits."

Shocked, I sat numbly looking at David, almost reeling at the story he had just told and how clearly it related to my own experience at the cemetery. It was also cross verification for a psychic reading Kingdon Brown had done for me three years before. Kingdon had said, "You were part of a large group, or tribe, who have reincarnated together again and again . . . but you were all wiped out . . . all wiped out at once. I don't understand, for I do not believe it was a natural calamity, but you all died together. In this life you are reuniting once again in Arizona. You have already met many of this group, and you will continue over the next few years to meet many more. They are coming from all over the country, and yours is a common bond and tie. Great strength can be achieved through this union."

My conversation with David now drifted to a discussion of metaphysical concepts. At one point I asked him a difficult question, and he leaned back to reflect. His eyes glazed over, his pupils enlarged, and in a totally different voice, he asked in heavily accented English, "Would you mind an interruption from an old friend?" I was talking directly with Wassily Kandinsky, as I did so often. Every Thursday morning for several weeks I had been meeting with David in his Prescott art studio to tape our metaphysical discussions. As David painted, he would go in and out of trance, and sometimes, while he was explaining a concept, Kandinsky would suddenly come through.

After Kandinsky answered the question, I asked him, "Can you provide me with any insight as to th psychic occurrences David and I both experienced in Mexico? Also, do you know anything about some ancient books I'm supposed to find and get together?"

"I'm surprised you haven't figured it out on your own," he replied. "What you are now doing and the concepts we have been discussing over the last several weeks are the basis of the books. You have already begun. In your Teotihuacan incarnation you had this knowledge. It was recorded and also painted upon the walls of the structure that stood adjacent to the Pyramid of the Sun. Changes in governing structures caused you to fear the misuse of this knowledge, just as you do now. So, in the past you painted over the murals, disguising their true meanings, and you and others destroyed the records."

Kandinsky named some acquaintances who were part of this conspiracy. Sipping some of David's coffee, he continued, "There were many others whom you have met and will continue to meet. You had far more knowledge at that time than you have in your present life, but you are rapidly opening yourself once again. A pact was made, in what is now called Teotihuacan, that all of you would reassemble every seven hundred years to present this information once again. You have reincarnated together many times, but conditions have not always been conducive to the presentation of these concepts. It is time once more to offer this understanding to those who have the ability to receive it."

Thankfully, we can't usually see around the corners of time or know the full breadth and depth of our own karmic responsibility to self and socie- ty. Metaphysics teaches that through your karmic experiences you form the character required to fulfill your destiny. You always have the free will to ignore this destiny, but to do so is to waste a valuable incarnation.

"I just don't get dharma," said Kevin Cavell, an art director and longtime friend from Phoenix who was visiting the mountains for the weekend. We sat on the front porch on a sunny fall afternoon, surrounded by color-splashed mountains.

"Supposedly, if you listen to your inner direction, you can't help but fulfill your dharma, so why worry about it?" I said.

"What's your dharma?" he asked.

"I have a dharmic direction of philosophy combined with a soul goal to provide support," I said.

"Soul goal? Come on, Richard, spell it out for me from the bottom up," he said.

"Okay, go on inside and lie down on the couch. I'll lead you through a process that will allow you to experience it," I said, and went to find the notes on dharma I had received in automatic writing. I directed Kevin through the deep breathing exercise and induced a deep hypnotic sleep.

"All right, now relax and be open to all awareness flowing into your mind. There are seven general dharmic directions, and I contend that it is your purpose to explore one of these directions in combination with a particular soul goal. First we'll explore your dharmic direction, and then we'll explore your soul goal. Now concentrate on the seven directions as I describe them.

"One is *workforce,* and this path includes the majority of general occupations, as well as homemakers.

"Two is *military,* and includes soldiers, police, and militia.

"Three is *service,* and includes most religious workers, as well as those in the medical profession, social services, and welfare.

"Four is *creativity,* and includes artists, writers, poets, musicians, actors, and entertainers.

"Five is *science,* and includes medical researchers, scientists, and space technologists.

"Six is *philosophy,* and includes all who present theories about why man does what he does and how to end suffering.

"Seven is *government,* and includes anyone elected to office.

"Now, open to higher awareness and perceive your own dharmic direction in vivid detail. You may or may not already be following this direction, but regardless of your present path, it is time to perceive this awareness. Which is your predestined direction: workforce, military, service, creativity, science, philosophy, or government? Perceive the direction and everything of importance in regard to this direction. Let this awareness come in on the count of three . . . one, two, three."

I remained quiet, allowing Kevin time to attain his own awareness. His body was stiff, as if frozen in position, but his eyelids fluttered as he observed his own internal images. As I gazed past the plants and stained glass, out through the picture window, twilight was tossing long shadows across Spruce Mountain. An occasional yellow leaf drifted down through the pastoral scene.

"All right, Kevin, now call out to your guides and Masters, and to highly evolved and loving entities on the other side who can provide you with additional awareness of your destiny. Call out silently, and receive this loving assistance. Hear your inner voice across the universe and back to you."

several minutes before asking Kevin me what he was experiencing.

that my dharmic direction is very soft and far away.

"Then I began to see fantasylike scenes of several people painting a huge mural on the side of a building. I knew I was one of them . . . an intense young man with a black mustache. My shirt was off and my sweating body was covered with different colors of paint. Suddenly soldiers came riding up on horses and shot us all. There was a momentary flash of panic, and then I was there, but I wasn't. I was above the situation and could see my body lying on the ground."

"What did you learn from your guides and Masters?" I asked.

"All I got was one sentence that echoed through my mind. It said, 'You used your art to protest social injustice.'" Still in a deep hypnotic trance, Kevin lay on the couch, eyes closed, speaking to me.

"All right, Kevin, I want you to totally let go of this, and we are going to explore something else. In addition to having chosen one of seven dharmic directions prior to your birth, I contend that you also chose one of seven basic soul goals. You can have more than one soul goal, but one will be most important, the next second in importance, and so on. Karmically, you have definite priorities regarding your life goals.

"The first goal is *to attain knowledge;* specifically knowledge which, when attained on a soul level, becomes wisdom. For example, you might desire direct knowledge of a trait, such as humility, devotion, persistence, sacrifice, selflessness, or perseverance.

"The second goal is *to open spiritually.* This means the integration of spiritual awareness into your dharmic direction.

"The third goal is *to achieve inner harmony.* This means to be involved with your life and the fulfillment of your dharma while at the same time attaining balance and peace of mind.

"The fourth goal is *to attain fame or power*

fame and power are karmic rewards and offer unique opportunities to communicate awareness and exert leadership.

"The fifth goal is *to learn acceptance,* which can be summarized as an awareness of 'what is, is.' It is your resistance to 'what is' that causes your suffering.

"The sixth goal is *to provide support.* This could amount to the encouragement and support of another individual in the accomplishment of a jointly shared dharmic direction, or support of a religious or philosophical belief or other cause.

"The seventh goal is *to develop a talent.* Talents are developed over many lifetimes, so the goal could be in the beginning, intermediate, or advanced stage of creative pursuit.

"And now, again, open to higher awareness. Your guides and Masters are right there with you, and it's time to perceive your primary soul goal in vivid detail. You may or may not be already working on the development of this goal, but regardless of your present path, it is time to attain this understanding."

Again I was quiet for several minutes before asking Kevin to speak up about what he was receiving.

"I'm to learn acceptance through my work. In Spain, I used my art as a political weapon and created great unrest. It's a reincarnational pattern over many lifetimes. Today, in the agency, I fight the account executives, forcing my ideas on them even when I know it isn't in the best interests of the client. I also create hateful political cartoons that are often publised in a weekly Tempe newspaper. One of my soul goals is to attain knowledge . . . the dge of humility. I have to learn that my ng is so, doesn't make it so." Slowly, le down Kevin's cheeks, so I uggestion that he find joy in

"I think I need to go out and walk around for a while," he finally said, after sitting silently for several minutes. I nodded, and watched from my chair as he walked across the leaf-strewn yard and down the dirt road toward the creek.

Tracy prepared dinner, and we didn't talk any more about metaphysics until late that evening. Freshly cut oak logs crackled in the fireplace as Kevin and Tracy sipped wine and I held a steaming mug of Jack Daniel's and coffee, waiting for it to cool.

"How do soulmates fit into your dharma?" Kevin asked.

"To me, all important relationships are soulmate relationships," I said. "But, based on my research, there are three kinds of soulmates. The first are *karmic companions*—two people who are destined to be together in order to confront unlearned lessons from past lives. These karmic-companion relationships seem to be karmically structured in one of three ways: locked in—the two people must remain together to resolve their conflicts; open-ended—the outcome of the relationship depends on the ability of each of the partners to learn and grow; or destined to end—for the opportunities for individual growth that the parting provides. If the two people can let go with love instead of hostility, they've learned their lesson. If not, they'll be back together in a future life for another round.

"The second kind of soulmate relationship is based on a *dharmic bond*—soulmates who share a goal. Everything I said about karmic companions applies here, but the couple combines their energies to accomplish a joint task. Depending on the karmic structuring, the predestined obligation will be fulfilled when the goal is either launched, established, or fully achieved. From then on the couple's future depends on their level of awareness and how they set up the relationship: whether they choose one that is locked in, open-ended, or destined to end.

"Third are *counterpart soulmates,* or *twin flames.* These are loving, supportive relationships in which the couple share their lives without conflict. Although problems might arise, they won't be with the soulmate. The couple has probably attained very close or matching vibrational rates. They harmonize, and the relationship is a karmic reward."

In the kitchen, dishes rattled as Tracy heated up some pie for dessert. "What kind of soulmates are you and Tracy?" Kevin asked.

"Well, although our relationship was certainly pre-destined, we don't get along well enough to be twin flames," I said, and laughed. "Considering my writing and the work we're doing together, probably dharmic-bond soulmates. Maybe it also has something to do with a child. We've picked up and cross-verified an Indian incarnation that involved her son by another man, a child I accepted and raised."

After spending time together and then living together for two years, Tracy and I got married for all the wrong reasons. I asked myself if it would be easier to get married than to go through the pain of parting. It's not that I didn't love her. I had grown to love her, but I wasn't passionately "in love" with her. I opted for the easy answer, which might appear to have been a mistake but, from a karmic perspective, was exactly what we both needed to experience.

In 1976 my book, *You Were Born Again to Be Together,* was published by Pocket Books. It attracted a lot of national attention and brought me invitations to appear on major TV talk shows. Tracy and I moved back to Scottsdale in 1977, and Travis Adam Sutphen was born on August 4 of that year. *Past Lives, Future Loves* came out in 1978. Valley of the Sun, a small publishing company I'd founded in 1968, was growing rapidly as the result of the publicity and media attention generated by my metaphysical books. I created a line of hypnosis tapes, the first of their kind, and they sold well as a mail order item. It was obvious from the way Tracy was spending money that I had to focus my energy on what produced the most income, which meant I could no longer take months off to write a book for just a small advance and semiannual royalties. The decision to conduct seminars on the road was a profitable one, but it only increased the pressures on our relationship.

Business got better, but Tracy and I got worse. She wanted to travel to exotic places several times a year; I didn't. I wanted to stay home, relax, and read at least one day out of each weekend; she didn't. I liked conducting the seminars and interacting with the participants; she grew to hate it. She wanted me to dress up; to me, dressed-up meant clean faded Levi's. I liked coffee shops and Mexican dives; she liked gourmet restaurants. We compromised as best we could until she found someone more like her, and then we divorced.

CHAPTER FOUR

Malibu, California
1983

Alone in my living room, I sipped Jack Daniel's and tracked the sun's slow descent through the mist into the Pacific. The Channel Islands emerged through the hazy glow of an incandescent pink sky, and a beam from the nearby lighthouse swept the January twilight, disappearing and reappearing. Soft lute music on the stereo enhanced the sound of the waves rolling and breaking on the beach below. A cool, salty breeze filled the room, and the flames in the fireplace tossed dancing reflections on the glass doors that opened onto the deck.

To capture the best possible views of the sea, houses built on Malibu hillsides are usually constructed with the living room and kitchen on the second floor. The cedar-shake exterior of my one-year-old home wrapped around the deck and then extended inside, along the fireplace wall in the living room. After only twelve months, you could already see how the outside shingles had weathered from their exposure to the sun and salt air.

The phone rang, and I let the answering machine take the call. "Richard, I know you're there," said

Christine's familiar voice through the tinny little speaker. "I'm at the studio and we've run into a snag."

I picked up the phone. "It's Sunday. Why are you working on the weekend?"

"It was the only time Roark had been available to experiment with a technique I want to use. But I need you to look at it," she said.

"Thirty minutes," I said. "I've got to shave and clean up."

Unseen Influences, my third book for Pocket, was now on bookstore shelves. I maintained a regular schedule of seminars in fifteen to twenty cities a year, and Valley of the Sun Publishing was proving very successful. In the fall of 1980 I moved my headquarters from Arizona to California. Living on the outskirts of Los Angeles offered many advantages, and fulfilled fantasies I'd had since my college days at L.A.'s Art Center School, when my classmates and I had partied on Malibu beaches. Now, standing on my deck years later, I could almost see the cove at the end of Westward Beach where I'd lost my virginity to one of the school's photo models.

Today my life centered around my work, my five-year-old son Travis, and a party circuit that consisted primarily of writers, psychics, and show business people. Since moving to California, I'd lived for a few months with a sexy ex-dealer from Florida. After several years of helping to run six-figure amounts of marijuana through the Keys, her psychic senses finally told her to get out. In response to my strong anti-drug position, she insisted, "I'm balancing my karma by contributing large sums of money to liberal causes."

There were many short-term romances, but by the beginning of 1983 I was feeling less and less need to date, or even to find a permanent relationship. I'd go to parties alone, and often come home alone too. For the first time that I could remember, I was quite content to be alone with myself.

Work kept me grounded, and new hypnosis tapes and a magazine about reincarnation were my priorities. Valley of the Sun Publishing, with a staff of twelve, was located in a converted motel/office building in the heart of Malibu's business district on the Pacific Coast Highway. Actor Dustin Hoffman owned the building, and Burt Reynolds lived across the street. My office manager, Jan Wright, hired her roommate, Christine Conrad, to do some temporary secretarial work for us. "She's a free-lance film producer who's between assignments, and she's also getting a divorce. She needs the money, and we need the help," Jan explained.

Christine, an Ali McGraw lookalike with a feisty personality, in happier days had helped her husband create and market the horror film *The Howling*. She'd worked in post production at Robert Altman's Lion Gate Films at Goldwyn Studios, and had a long string of credits for producing television commercials. Our talks about incorporating video into the Valley of the Sun line of tapes grew into long lunches and a deep friendship. Christine was soon handling coordination for all my seminars, and we spent days at a time together on the road, traveling from city to city. In an Atlanta, Georgia, hotel room we came up with the concept for *The No Effort Subliminal Weight Loss Video*, and in a Malibu studio that specialized in MTV rock-music videos, we created the first video to offer subliminal programming.

Christine and Roark McGonigle, owner of Tower of 6 Video, were studying a wall of monitors when I walked into the production studio. "Look at this effect," Christine said excitedly, snapping her fingers at Roark. The main monitor crackled to life with music and surrealistic images of galloping horses and riders in colorful Arabic attire.

"I'm really impressed," I said. As the video opens, an overweight woman is imagining the dreamlike experiences enjoyed by a beautiful young woman with a perfect body. The visuals varied, ranging from subliminal images of a refrigerator blowing open and garbage spewing out to shots of the woman playing with rabbits on a fantasy set. Visual suggestions were flashed on the screen at a brain rate conducive to extreme relaxation. They said things like: "Every day you become thinner," "Eat smaller portions," "Eat only healthy food," "Stick to your diet," and "Eat only at mealtime."

In addition, we psychoacoustically modified and synthesized my verbal suggestions and projected them in the same chord and frequency as the background music, making the suggestions part of the music. The result was a thirty-minute, three-level subliminal program that would be extremely effective.

The actress we used was blond beauty Lisa Lindgren, a regular on "General Hospital." By the time Lisa realized she had signed on to act in a very weird, low-budget, experimental video that might get a lot of publicity, she asked her father-in-law, a lawyer, to make sure that her photo did not appear on the tape sleeve.

Later, Christine and I had dinner at The Sand Castle, a cozy hideaway behind a guard gate at Paradise Cove. The dark wood walls were covered with nautical objects, from a ship's wheel to harpoons. The seaward windows looked out on the long arm of a fishing pier that extended almost due south into the Pacific. The lights of a few pleasure boats at anchor rose and fell on the waves, flickering in a black void. Sitting in the deep, red leather booth, I played with the ship's rigging and the ropes on the walls.

"What do you know about Alan Vaughan?" Christine asked, after we'd ordered drinks.

"He used to be the editor of *Psychic* magazine, published in San Francisco," I said. "When he applied for the editor/writer job, I hired him because he was the best qualified."

"God, he's a space cadet." She laughed.

"According to Alan, the Central Premonitions Registry in New York claims he is the world's most successful psychic predictor," I replied.

"What did he do to deserve that honor?"

"I think all psychics are invited to submit their predictions to the agency, and they keep track of who is correct and who isn't."

"So it could be that Alan simply submitted a lot more predictions than anyone else?"

I shrugged my shoulders.

Christine continued, "He got to me the other day. I was sitting on the floor, assembling a press release, when I noticed he was staring at me. He said, 'I have the strangest feeling of déjà vu. Years ago I had a dream about working here in this exact room with you. You had black hair and were surrounded by stacks of papers. In the dream, I think you had a large black dog named Tiny Tim.'"

"I thought your dog was named Chinaman?" I said.

"True, but Chinaman is large and black, and Tiny Tim used to be my nickname!"

The waitress arrived with our drinks, and Christine ordered broiled orange roughy; I ordered mahi mahi. "Was there any more to the Alan story?" I asked.

"Yeah. He brought this large dream journal to work with him on Friday. He records all his meaningful dreams in journals. This dream dated back to 1970, and in it he answered an ad for editorial work on a metaphysical publication. He got the job, and I was also one of the people working there."

Goose bumps ran up and down my arms as I raised my glass for a toast. "To destiny!" We both laughed.

A few days later, at the office, I went over the story with Alan. "Does your dream substantiate predestination, Alan? Thirteen years ago I certainly wasn't planning to be in Malibu publishing this magazine."

"No," he replied. "It was one of many probable futures. It just happened to be the one that worked out. Four years before I met my wife Diane, a psychic gave me precise information about the woman I would marry, including her professional background, involvements, and regional interests. The psychic was totally accurate."

"So, Diane was one of many probably futures?" I said.

"She was my primary destiny," he replied. "Either of us could have exercised free will and chosen not to accept it."

"Relationships and the idea of destiny manipulating us on the chessboard of life have always been my favorite topics of metaphysical investigation," I said. I knew that shared past lives are the prerequisite for an important relationship in this one. And people appear to come together and to part according to an unseen plan, their union being either a reward or an opportunity for learning.

In November 1982, Alan had done a psychic reading for me, predicting that "You are going to meet a beautiful, lean lady with long black hair very soon— around Christmas time or shortly thereafter. She will be very important to you and I think you'll live together." It was now a little after Christmas, and I'd met a lean, dark-haired lady in Fresno while conducting a seminar, but she didn't intrigue me half as much as Christine, who was already involved with someone else.

Actress/author Susan Strasberg had recently prepared a numerology reading for me. She said, "My, my, Richard, you have a very important relationship forthcoming, and in 1984 you will remarry." I nodded attentively but I was laughing inside. Marriage just didn't seem appropriate for me, although I love living within a family.

Lorraine Laahs, an Encino-based psychic, often called me to supply a running commentary on my future. "I see walls going up, building . . . and a dark-haired woman with Indian blood is involved."

Finally, my astrologer, Barbara May, told me of a predestined meeting that was "very strong" in my chart.

After being around psychics for twenty years, I know how easy it is for their predictions to be off or for situations to be misread, so I had never given their readings much credence. But at the same time, I couldn't help but wonder to what degree our personal movies are already written and produced. I had recently read Richard Bach's *Illusions* aloud to Christine while we waited in the Chicago airport. In the book, Richard and Don, the "reluctant Messiah," talked about life as a self-produced film. You experience your movie sequentially, frame by frame, as you do in a theater. Yet as the book says, at the same time you are watching, or experiencing, any sequence, "It's all finished and complete—beginning, middle, end are all there that same second, the same millionth of a second. The film exists beyond the time that it records."

The Ultimate Frontier, a book by Eklal Kueshana, addresses the concept of prearranged primary relationships as a "union of minds" we build together prior to incarnating. According to the author, this union constitutes a third entity, or etheric corporation, which is a binding mutual pact that "attracts you to one another and holds you together."

While in Scottsdale, Arizona, in February 1983 to conduct a training seminar for professional hypnotists, I had dinner with Brad and Francie Steiger. That night Francie told me for the first time that she'd been certain my previous relationship was destined to end. "Do you know why you had to go to California, Richard?"

"No, Francie. Why?"

"For very important contacts that could only be made there. And you have a few more to make. I've had two dreams about you lately."

After the seminar I drove back to California alone. While crossing the desert I started to think about planning a party when I returned to Malibu. Because I lived alone, I gave few parties, but the urge was very strong, and this one seemed important. I quickly wrote and designed an invitation as I drove. The excuse would be to announce our new subliminal weight-loss video; I would show it for the first time that evening. About a hundred people from the metaphysical and entertainment worlds were invited, as well as my office staff. Christine offered to help me prepare the food.

On the night of February 19, 1983, the house was full of exciting people—the party was a definite success. I had just finished talking with actress Terry Moore, a contender for a portion of the enormous Howard Hughes estate, and had walked into the kitchen to refill my drink when I spotted metaphysical author Jess Stearn making his way through the crowd. He was accompanied by a couple of his male friends and a black-haired, emerald-eyed, lean and lovely young woman.

My throat contracted and I could hardly breathe. She was the most beautiful woman I'd ever seen. She was dressed in a red Western shirt, skintight black jeans, and red cowboy boots. "Richard," Jess said, "this is Tara McKean. She's visiting from Sedro Woolley, Washington."

"Hi," she said shyly.

Tara's smiling eyes hid a sensuous flame that crackled above the sounds of the party. There was no one else in the room. There had never been anyone else. "I'm glad you could come," I said, a faint tremor in my voice, as though some deep, long-forgotten emotion had been touched.

Tara offered to get Jess a drink. Halfway across the kitchen she turned to look at me—a look that will linger forever in my mind, a look that will probably flash before my inner eye for incarnations to come, a look of recognition and confusion that reflected everything I was feeling. If I had listened, I would probably have heard the voices of our spirit guides echoing across the universe, congratulating each other on a masterful job of maneuvering.

While the crowd milled about I talked with Tara, as part of one group, then another. Eventually we were alone for a few minutes. She had moved to Washington only four months earlier, but before that had lived in Southern California for several years. She'd been a Hollywood model and worked in security for two years at the Warner Brothers/Columbia Burbank film studios. "When the 'Dukes of Hazzard' cars went flying through the air, I'd make sure no bystanders got killed," she said, laughing.

The fast-paced Hollywood lifestyle had little appeal for her, though, so she had piled her furniture into a U-Haul truck, loaded her two horses into a trailer she towed behind it, and drove with her six-year-old son William to Washington, where she rented a small ranch on the outskirts of Sedro Woolley.

"Why Sedro Woolley?" I asked, as I noticed her beautiful obsidian earrings.

"It's quiet, clean, and cheap to live there," she said. "And it's beautiful, too."

"When do you have to go back?"

"Tomorrow morning," she said. I felt my heart sink.

We talked about many things. Since she had come with Jess, I assumed that she was interested in metaphysics, but she knew very little about the subject or even about Jess's work. He was a longtime family friend, she said. Her primary interest was horses, and since I'd owned horses for thirteen years in Arizona, we had a lot in common. My son Travis was five, and we exchanged kid stories. But then other people gathered around us and there was little chance to talk privately. As the evening wore on we continued to watch each other, and I realized I'd better open the door to further contact soon, before she left.

Tara was standing with a large group of people when I walked up, took her by the hand and said, "I have something I want to show you." I escorted her downstairs to my bedroom, where we could speak in private. "Can I call you in Washington?" I asked tentatively. She smiled, nodded, and wrote her address and phone number on the back of an envelope that lay on the dresser.

"I almost didn't come tonight," she said. "I spent an exhausting day visiting friends out in Green Valley and didn't get back to Jess's house until late. He handed me the party invitation when I came in the door and asked me if I wanted to go. What I really wanted was to just sit back and relax, but I found myself staring at your cartoon invitation for at least ten minutes, feeling, for some reason, compelled to come here."

"I wish you didn't have to go back tomorrow," I said.

"Me too, but I have to get back for William," she

explained. "He's been staying with friends for a week."

Two days later I called her in Washington. "Tara, I realize we don't know each other, but I'd sure like to get to know you, and it would be pretty hard to date at this distance. Would you consider taking a vacation with me? We could bring the kids along . . . I was thinking about Hawaii for ten days."

There was a silence on the other end of the line. Then she asked: "Are you serious?"

"Yes," I responded timidly.

There was another long pause. "Yes, I think so. When were you planning to leave?"

"In a few days."

When Tara and William arrived at LAX a few days later, Travis and I were there to meet them. "I don't believe I'm doing this," she said. "I've never done anything like this in my life."

William and Travis got along like brothers. When they were finally asleep for the night, Tara and I sat on the floor in front of the fireplace, drinking wine and talking about everything except what was really on our minds. Finally, when it was time to go to bed, I said, "We don't have to do anything. I know we hardly know each—" But Tara placed her index finger on my lips, silencing me. In the bedroom I lighted several candles, and we undressed wordlessly, facing each other. She stood before me smiling, a heart-rending tenderness in her gaze; she was beautiful, naked, and more desirable than heaven itself. The anticipation was almost unbearable.

The sound of crashing waves filled the bedroom as we slipped beneath the covers. My arms encircled her. As our warm flesh touched, she sighed and buried her face in the corded muscles of my neck. My breathing was uneven as I explored the hollows of her back with one hand while massaging her small buttocks with the other. Then her breath fanned my face, and soon my tongue was exploring the recesses of her mouth. Our kisses were exquisitely tender and gentle, and the next moment, intensely urgent and reckless. My hand seared a path down her abdomen to the swell of her hips and she pushed her body against mine, lifting her hips in a sensuous invitation. We both breathed in deep soul-drenching drafts. Then, in a flood of uncontrollable joy, I was inside her, consumed in waves of ecstasy.

I looked down into her eyes, dancing in the candlelight, and cupped her face gently in my hands. "We both knew, didn't we?"

She smiled and nodded. "Yes, we both knew."

Later, lying together in the passion-soaked bed, we listened to the ocean and held each other as if it would have to last a lifetime.

CHAPTER FIVE

Maui, Hawaii;
Sedona, Arizona
1983

We started each day with steaming mugs of Kona coffee and fresh papaya laced with lime juice as we sat on the balcony of the Sands of Kahana apartments, overlooking Kaanapali Beach. These laid-back days on Maui were dedicated to absorbing the sun and each other in an environment of rustling palm fronds, caressed by the warm island breezes mingled with the smell of Hawaiian Tropic tanning oil.

Splashing in the surf with our sons and chasing the lazily spinning Frisbee as it lured us in and out of the waves, we worked up a healthy appetite for the freshly caught fish sizzling on grills at the open-air restaurants. We toured the art galleries, went horseback and moped riding, and sat in the marina watching the orange and crimson sky fade to black.

Our nights were for making love, sometimes almost until dawn. Passion consumed me—I could not get enough of this beautiful woman, so gentle, yet with such inner strength and self-assurance. After producing six volumes of poetry, I hadn't written many new poems in years. Now, the flood of words wouldn't stop. "I was in love with you before I knew your last name," was the last line of one of those poems. And it was true.

"I was born in Seattle, Washington. When I was two years old, my family moved to California," Tara told me. We lay in the darkness, with a view of the sea and the bobbing lights of passing boats. As she spoke, I ran my fingers gently up and down her naked body. "I spent my childhood in the San Francisco Bay area, then later the San Joaquin Valley. When I was fifteen, the family moved to Anchorage, Alaska, where five generations of my mother's family still lived." There were often long pauses in our conversations while we stroked each other. "And if you keep doing that, Richard, the subject is going to get changed very soon." She sighed and laid her head on my chest.

"Scottish and English, huh?"

"Possibly a little Blackfoot Indian, too. It's a rumor that is supported by an old family photo. My grandfather told me about it, but my father doesn't accept it."

As I stroked Tara's beautiful long black hair I remembered the words of Lorraine Laahs, "a dark-haired woman with Indian blood is involved."

Tara told me about the prediction Jess Stearn had made three years earlier. During a psychic reading, Jess had said to her, "In time I will introduce you to the most important man in your life. I can see you standing, dressed in white, embracing this man on the patio of my Malibu beach house. You'll marry the man, Tara."

Tara's first marriage had quickly proved to be disastrous, and she was soon supporting herself by working in the family chiropractic clinic in Anchorage. In an attempt to improve her finances she took a job on the Alaska pipeline, at Sohio's base operations camp in Prudhoe Bay, Alaska, in the Arctic Circle, where the temperature averaged seventy degrees below zero. Although she was earning $1150 a week in 1978, after a year on the pipeline she wanted to return to the sunshine.

So Tara purchased a home in Ojai, California, signed with a Hollywood agency, and launched a successful modeling career while working with the film studios on a free-lance basis. For the next four years she lived in California, raising her son and trying to live with him as a family. The modeling and studio work led to an open invitation to the parties at the Playboy Mansion and Hollywood gatherings that proved to be, in her words, "too much of a good thing. You lose touch with reality . . . and with yourself, as well." Tara's values were in conflict with her career and she wanted out.

The sanctuary she had longed for was Sedro Woolley. There she found a small ranch to rent, which she and her son William shared with her cousin Erin. Her life centered around home, her horses, and the two cats. "I only dated men who lived as far away as Seattle or Vancouver because I didn't want a serious, close relationship," she explained.

Our conversation turned to dreams. "A couple of weeks before I met you, I had such a weird dream that I kept Erin awake half the night," Tara said. "Erin finally woke me about four A.M. and told me I'd been speaking a foreign language and chanting. I could only remember people dressed in robes and holding torches. And pyramids—I think I was on top of a huge, flat-topped pyramid."

Once back in Malibu, neither of us wanted to part. "Why don't you stay for another week, and we can fly to Seattle together?" I said. I was conducting a past-life therapy seminar in Seattle the next Saturday and one in Portland on Sunday. Tara agreed.

The week at home gave us more time to get to know each other. Until now, Tara had been unfamiliar with my work—although a vegetarian with an interest in astrology, she had never paid much attention to metaphysics. At four-thirty Tuesday morning the telephone rang to announce the start of a scheduled over-the-phone radio interview. I'd been awake for about fifteen minutes. "It's drive time in New Jersey, folks, and our guest today is a reincarnation specialist, live, all the way from Malibu, California. Good morning, Dick Sutphen. How's the weather in Malibu?"

Tara peeked out from under the covers. While I talked for ten minutes, she slipped out of bed and went up to the kitchen to fix a pot of coffee. She presented the steaming mug along with a smile, a kiss, and a sleepy-eyed question: "How often does this happen?"

"As often as my staff can line them up," I replied. "They generate a lot of book and tape sales."

Tara's first experience with a seminar participant occurred at the Seattle hotel where the workshop was being held. A woman approached us and introduced herself, explaining, "I'm a transsexual anorexic, and I'd like to talk with you about your research in this area." I glanced at Tara, who was watching wide-eyed.

"I've never even met a transsexual anorexic before, much less done any research in that area," I replied.

I heard Tara mumbling something about an "interesting career" as the woman walked away. But as I soon learned, if there was ever a soul who took naturally to metaphysics, it was Tara McKean.

Although we eventually said our good-byes at the Seattle airport, our feelings for each other had grown so much stronger that I easily talked her into finding someone to care for the horses for a while so she could return to Malibu with her son, some more clothes, and her two cats.

By May we both knew we never wanted to be apart, and we decided to live together. Tara flew back to

Washington to pack and prepare for the movers, and I flew up a few days later to meet her and help trailer the horses south.

The drive south along the Pacific coast to Northern California was beautiful, relaxing, and uneventful. The second night we stayed at a motel in a rural area, and the next morning we fed and watered the horses, then exercised them. But just as we were about to put them back in the trailer, Ojai, Tara's three-year-old part-Arabian, overreacted to a small noise. He reared, freeing his lead rope, and off he went at a full gallop, over the motel shrubbery, through the parked cars, then in a huge circle through the oat field next door.

Having owned horses most of my adult life, I sighed, shook my head and grabbed another lead rope, expecting to spend the next hour chasing Ojai. I looked at Tara, but she simply watched calmly, a smile on her face, as the horse continued to circle, uprooting a few of the motel's shrubs each time he misjudged a jump. I was just about to start after him when she shook her head no. After he'd completed a few more circles, she put two fingers to her mouth and gave an ear-shattering whistle. Ojai immediately slowed to a trot and headed straight for her, walked up to her and began to rub his nose up and down on her jacket.

"He was just looking for an excuse to freak out," she said, leading the tired horse into the trailer.

"I guess we all do that once in a while, don't we?" I responded. And as we drove through the California countryside, I recalled some of the times I'd created such excuses, always to avoid taking responsibility for my actions. I wouldn't feel quite right or justified in doing what I wanted to do, so I'd had to find a way to avoid the guilt.

In my seminars I talk a great deal about self-processing. Once exposed to the concept and technique, it becomes a part of your life. You find yourself

automatically asking yourself questions about everything you do. The goal is *clarity of intent.* Obviously,
one important question is, "Am I creating an excuse
to do what I want to do?" And if the answer is yes, the
next question might be, "What do I need to do so that
I can do what I want without losing self-esteem?"

Tara adapted easily to the rock-and-roll lifestyle of
the road. With her support and encouragement, even
doing the seminars became a pleasure. I was scheduled to offer my first psychic seminar in Sedona,
Arizona—a small town in the central part of the state,
where majestic red-rock mountains and sculptured
buttes rise from the desert like the spiritually uplifting
vortex forces that abound there. I'd described my
experiences in these energy vortexes in *You Were Born
Again to Be Together,* and the book had created a great
deal of interest in the New Age. The town has never
been the same since.

Over two hundred participants came from thirty-
eight states to attend the three-day event, which I was
scheduled to lead with Alan Vaughan. Any audience,
properly prepared, is capable of demonstrating psychic abilities, and I counted on the highly charged
environment of Sedona to greatly increase the odds of
success. That Friday morning, after a short introduction, I boldly announced that we would start with a
telepathy session in which each person would be
hypnotically chakra-linked to a partner they didn't
know.

"You have permission to be psychic in here," I said
to the hypnotized participants. "I am expecting you to
be psychic, and we're going to begin with some
telepathic exercises. I want you to focus your concentration on the person you picked as a partner. Again,
capture their essence in your mind. Do this very
vividly, and imagine where they are sitting in relationship to your own chair."

After directing the chakra link-up, I said, "Your top three chakras are now connected and it is time to perceive powerful, accurate telepathic impressions about your partner's life. The impressions will begin to flow into your mind on the count of three. One, two, three."

The participants were given several minutes to receive. Tara and I sat at the podium, holding hands, cupping a crystal, and mentally merging our energies to telepathically send them three separate symbols. "Now, Tara and I are going to send you three symbols which you will accurately receive and remember. We will send them as we see them drawn on the paper before us and as they might appear in manifest form."

The session was an unqualified success. At least eighty-five to ninety percent of the participants psychically received the first symbol, which actually combined two separate images. More than half received the next two symbols. Statistically, that kind of result is highly improbable. And the group did as well telepathically reading their partners. The seminar was off to a flying start, and I knew the automatic writing, energy transfer, and psychometry sessions would work equally well.

Alan Vaughan was scheduled to work with the group in other PSI explorations, but as an unplanned special event, he unexpectedly channeled an entity named Li Sung for the first time. Although Alan had been a professional psychic for many years, he had never done any verbal channeling. Clearly, the intense energy of the environment that was affecting seminar participants so powerfully was also affecting him. As Alan stood on stage, in trance, Li Sung began speaking through him. It was a thought-provoking experience for everyone involved.

On Saturday afternoon seminar participants went out to explore the energy vortexes. Alan offered Tara and me a private session with Li Sung. In our darkened motel room he entered into an altered state of consciousness. His face contorted just a little and then a strange voice began to speak in broken English:

"You are together because you have chosen to be. It was in Roman times, in school, when you came. You said, I elect to come to meet this entity because of eight hundred years of being together before. Mongolia was the first time. Let me just say briefly what these times be in the past. In Mongolia, you [Tara] were shoveling soot from the fires. He was male in that lifetime. He was brave . . . rode horses. He was your idol, but he ignored you. You were only a little girl. You said 'I love him,' but he did not know you were there.

"Next time maybe. Next time maybe. I will skip a few lifetimes. Coming to Rome. Eh! Again female. You were female, Tara. You pledged celibacy. You pledged to be virgin. And you were virgin. He was not true. He said, 'I want to be your friend,' but he wanted your body. He loved you in ways that were not possible. He was soldier, a centurion. There was an affair of the heart where there should not have been an affair of the heart. You could not give your body to him; you languished. He did not feel at all guilty. He only wanted you. There was a child . . . not your child, but a child destined to be among you. The child had wanted you to be his parents, but you elected to be celibate priestess. The child could not come through you, so the child came through another woman and attached itself quickly to you and this man. But still it was not fulfilling. Then you decided you will live five lives more, to develop understanding between the two of you.

"Indian. You were American Indian. In what is now New Mexico, I think. Then he was brave. You loved. He was mated to other woman, yet you loved him.

You met behind bushes. In that lifetime, he very nice to you. Finally. First time. But yet there could not be bond of matrimony because he married to powerful woman. He must be faithful to woman. Lesson not learned.

"Next time. First time, Nova Scotia . . . or where people wear lots of clothes. They are cold. Much fur. Maybe Mongolia again. I do not see place, I only see clothes. Aaaah, this time you a man, Tara. This time you decide to claim power. He listen to you. This woman [Richard] younger than you. You seduce this young maiden. You have your way with this maiden. You powerful, and you love this maiden. But you feel more in love with power. Maiden have babies, many babies. Maiden love babies. You could not care about children. You go away to fight war. You leave maiden with five babies. This one [Richard] have life of great dedication, great sacrifice, bringing up babies all alone. Beautiful karma earned here. You [Tara] disappear.

"Next life, Mexico. Then a South American environment. Aaahh, you are beautiful maiden now, Tara, much as you are now. Beautiful maiden. And you are balanced in your understanding of life. You have understanding of way to please man with love and wisdom. You cultivate wisdom. This one, he appears again. He is your own age. He is a youth, very ambitious. He wants to rule. He wants to lead army. And yet he has not to fight . . . he has to think. The ardor of his youth catches your heart. You become truly in love. Is there matrimony, you ask? No. There should have been, but there was not. Yet this was your first love. It was unfair. The universe did not cooperate this time. There was a moment, in a garden filled with tropical scents. You bade good-bye. You beautiful maiden, he earnest young military adviser. Tears were shed. You said, 'Never more, never more will I become so upset with my emotions.' He married another woman. He went to another province. He became a big, big man in another province. He had much power, but you never saw each other again.

"That most powerful lifetime influencing present now. This is to be arranged again, in better circumstances. This time you come. You have been married. You have child. He has been married. Children he has, but that is not the meeting point for you now. You have only to choose for love. You have not to raise families more unless you want to. You have not to create positions of power. You need only love each other in the way you yearned for eight hundred years. This will be possible because you have paid in advance for the opportunity. Do you not feel certain kinds of understandings? See Richard . . . the Richard now. Warlike before, now he is gentle. He has changed; he has understood and learned. You were beautiful last time, Tara. You are beautiful this time because last time you understood, so you can be same again. You are here not to worry but to help and love each other. You are offered great opportunity to get what you need.

"Questions in my mind: Will you do properly in this connection, in this wonderful preorganized commitment? Tara, that is yet undecided by you. You have not made commitment. Richard—he does not know for sure, yet he wants to. He says, 'If you make commitment, perhaps I will, but I am not sure right now.' You [Tara] need to reverse a karmic pattern from the past when he rules you, when he paid no attention to you. Remember that lifetime? You have to readjust that. Now he listen to you. You treat him kindly, however, you tell him a thing or two. You good for him. He learn from you. You do not believe, Tara, I know. I know. That is not important because you are what you are and who you are . . . the many who's that you are. That is the important thing. Disregard what I say if you choose, but control him. It is your duty to give him sense of responsibility, sense of loving, sense of being. I know not word . . . sorry, I know not English word.

"Richard, you were a scoundrel, sir," Li Sung said.

"When was that?" I said.

"Ah-hah! You mean, 'How many times was that?' That's all right. Don't worry—you a good man now. Oh, my, my, my . . . what you have done in the past! I make no judgment; the word 'scoundrel' only means you interesting. You explore all boundaries. You want to be bad in as many ways as you can in order to find out what good is. That is the way we learn. Of course! You, sir, have brilliance. You have learned much from past lives. As the Vaughan body knows, you have investigated relationships because you realize that you have, as they say, 'fucked up' so many of them. That is why you want to make them better, and this is the best karma for you. You will bring understanding about this situation, the most important situation in human affairs. I do not like the word 'relationship.' That is too modern, too American. We prefer to talk about love and commitment, making desire known for a price of paying back with indeed more love. So, there is a balance. You brilliant man. You have much to teach because you have learned so much. And, by the same token, you have more to learn. But enough, they say, is enough. You have lived so many lives; surely, by now, you have grasped the truth. Tara teach you a thing or two.

"Tara does not know if she believes in past lives. It does not matter. Understanding past lives is not point; understanding what is between you is point. Permit me to say, sir, that you have extraordinary brilliance in this regard because it is finally come to you that a man, woman, child man, child woman, family, loves, is what makes human beings into people. You are sensitive to other people in profound ways. You give them love but you do not want love back. That would defeat your purpose. You give them understanding but you not want understanding back because that would defeat your purpose. Be content with your purpose. Tara, she help. She tell you thing or two.

"Tara has spent many lifetimes learning love. She knows how to give love. She rides like Indian princess on horse. Land that she loves . . . all she sees. Not just people, but the very land itself. She good mistress of land. Richard, you, sir, in future can choose what you want. But you want place, ranch, horses. You need that again. She need that again. She need that. She want that. She'll tell you what to do. You'll see. You need environment where you get close to land, and there must be much land. You and she, king and queen of land. You settle back on ranch, ride horses together. Animals, rocks, grass, and beauty. Indian presence must be there. If Indian presence not there, you cannot stay there. You resonate in environment. She will guide you to best place. Trust her. But time is perhaps not now. You finish business first. You do television. You communicate in California. Two more years, then you do what you wish."

Alan Vaughan sighed deeply, opened his eyes, and sat up erect in his chair. "Whew, that must have been some session," he said, obviously attempting to reorient to the real world. "Did Li Sung say anything interesting?"

Tara and I looked at each other and nodded in agreement. Although I hadn't told Alan, the day before, in a seminar session, I had self-induced a past-life regression along with the participants. For the first time I asked, "Have Tara and I been together before? If so, I want to go back to the lifetime most influencing our present incarnations."

The following, transcribed from recorded notes made immediately after my regressive experience, seems to relate to the South American life that Li Sung said was "the most powerful lifetime influencing the present."

I see a ridge sloping down to the sea. It overlooks a bay, and many small boats are anchored below. Along the ridge is a lattice-fenced walkway. About every hundred feet there is a tall, decorative, latticed archway. At a point about halfway down the ridge the walkway becomes a circle—obviously a viewing site overlooking the bay below. I am walking down the pathway with a beautiful young woman, and I know it is Tara. When we get to the circle, we are holding each other; we are very much in love. We have dark complexions and are both dressed formally. She is wearing her hair in an unusual style—braided into big circles on the side, with a portion falling freely and flaring out in the back; it is held by a very decorative comb.

When I ask where we are, I get an image of the top of South America, the area around Venezuela.

Later, looking at a map, I had a strong sense that it was Maracaibo, Venezuela, close to the huge bay or inland sea.

The next flashes are of us together in an elegant, Spanish-style home with very high ceilings, very formal. She lives here and we are having a discussion. I want her to leave with me but she doesn't want to go. I have an opportunity elsewhere—a job or assignment. Her family is very rich. The arched walkway is part of their estate, and it seems to be the late 1700s or early 1800s.

We both love each other, but I won't pass up the opportunity, and she won't leave the security of her home and family. We are both very sad for we know we will lose each other.

CHAPTER SIX

On the Road
1984–87

Tara and I were married on the deck of Jess Stearn's beach house in Malibu, California, March 2, 1984. She wore a simple white dress and held an armful of wildflowers. The sea breeze tossed her raven hair across her face as she said, "I will," and leaned into me, smiling from across the barriers of lifetimes past. The sea gulls laughed above and the surf pounded the sand below.

"I love you, my wife," I whispered, and kissed her deeply.

The ceremony was performed by New Age minister Dave Van Hooser at a time chosen by astrologer Barbara May. My oldest son, Scott, was my best man, LeNaeh Ashford was Tara's bridesmaid, and William and Travis stood beside us during the ceremony. Actress Diane Ladd filled the deck with beautiful flower arrangements. A few close friends, relatives, and my office staff attended.

After honeymooning at the Casa Marina Hotel in Key West, we settled back into the lifestyle we both loved. Tara attended a community college part-time, taking equine science classes to learn more about horses and breeding. Her quick mind and nearly photographic memory also helped her to master tarot, handwriting analysis, palmistry, and personology. Within a year she had attained a professional level of expertise in these psychic sciences.

For nearly two years we maintained houses in both Malibu and Scottsdale, Arizona, and northern Mexico was very much a part of our life. El Golfo de Santa Clara crowns the Sea of Cortez, and a forty-mile stretch of nearly deserted white sand beach became our home away from home. On long weekends, spring break, and summer vacations we'd run the dunes in our four-wheel drive, blow up hundreds of dollars worth of fireworks, and go skinny dipping in the tepid sea.

We coexisted with rattlesnakes, sand vipers, scorpions, cow killers, stingrays, jellyfish, and—with the quiet support of a long-barreled pistol—the macho American bikers. But by 1985 the Mexican government was sending soldiers with automatic weapons into the sleepy fishing village to protect the peasants from themselves. During the El Golfo Easter festivities, I noticed a soldier watching my wife, three of our children, and me. Eyeing us with open hatred, he fingered his assault rifle and searched for the remotest justification to express his hostility. That night, in my journal, I wrote: "Their misdirected hatred no longer lies below the surface. Today it dances in the sunlight to the beat of a ticking time bomb."

By 1986 we stopped going to Mexico and gave up the Scottsdale house to spend all our time in Malibu. The Phoenix valley was changing. To escape the midwestern winters, people by the thousands were leaving and moving to the desert, but once they arrived they wanted the desert to look more like the Midwest, so they built Tudor houses and planted green lawns surrounded by fake lakes. The humidity increased, and for the first time mosquitoes became routine. Community regulations multiplied, too, and developers seemed to rule greedy city councils that dreamed of governing great cities. Whenever we were in Arizona, I'd find myself waiting at the Circle K for the *Los Angeles Times* to arrive. Finally I wrote in my journal: "It's time to stay at the beach and accept the fact that the Midwest is a thousand miles closer than it used to be."

Hunter Shane Sutphen was born June 2, 1986, a joyful day in all our lives. If ever I were sure of a soul tie with one of my children, it was with Hunter. My psychic investigation revealed that he and I had been together as part of the same family in many prior lifetimes, even as mates. With a baby at home our lifestyle changed. We built a barn and bought an interest in a local tennis club; we seldom left Malibu, except to go on the road to conduct seminars.

Business was booming for Valley of the Sun Publishing; I developed a line of video-hypnosis tapes and expanded our network of retailers. Tara often encouraged me to write another book for Pocket Books, and that winter they accepted my proposal for *Predestined Love.*

I spent the first six months of 1987 writing the book. My editor had requested the manuscript by June 15, two weeks earlier than the original deadline, which meant working from dawn till midnight at my computer during early June.

For assistance I played the *Writer's Programming Tapes* I'd created specifically for professional writers. The subliminal sides provided background music while I was editing and rewriting, and at night I fell asleep listening to one of the hypnosis/sleep-programming sides, including "Revision & Rewriting," "Comprehensive Programming," "Increase Your Writing Speed & Productivity," and "A Nonfiction Book." I even threw in "A Successful Novel" and

"Successful Short Stories" from time to time, because I was recounting the case histories in fictionalized form.

The tapes helped a lot, but too much programming can be too much of a good thing. Soon I was being awakened in the middle of the night, usually about four A.M., by an inner voice suggesting changes I should make in the manuscript. I found that until I turned on the light and recorded these bits of information, I could not go back to sleep. The advice was always excellent, although I would have preferred to receive it during the day.

On Friday, June 12, the final manuscript was shipped express mail to my agent in New York City. I felt a great sense of relief as I went to bed that night, planning to sleep late the next morning. But around four A.M. my eyes opened wide and the voice in my head was so loud it seemed to fill our bedroom. I quickly looked around the dimly lit room. Tara was cuddled against me, sleeping soundly. "Hey, the book's done and I don't need any more help," I said softly.

"It's time for even more important communications," came the response.

"Oh, come on!"

"You are one of 25,000 people who reincarnated together to share your concepts with the world."

"I don't want to know about this now. I just want to sleep," I protested.

"Fourteen hundred years ago, in what you now call Teotihuacan, you all made a pact to return together. Today, the effects of your combined energy are being felt around the world."

"Teotihuacan? I haven't been into that for twelve years. Besides, I've been getting the books together. I just mailed the last one and I want to sleep."

"This is the only time of the night or day you are

directly receptive to our communications. Your use of the tapes has heightened your receptivity. Now write down what we have to tell you so you will remember it in the morning."

Knowing from experience that the only way to get back to sleep was to commit the communication to writing, I grudgingly sat up, turned on the table lamp, and found a pen in the nightstand drawer. The back of a large envelope was the only paper I could find to write on. "One of the 25,000 from Teotihuacan who made a pact to reincarnate together . . ." I scrawled sleepily.

"Are you telling me that all the current interest in metaphysics and the New Age is being generated by people reincarnated from this group?"

"There are many groups who share your ideas, but none of the others are as large. The present vibrational rate and circumstances on earth are ideal for this sharing."

"Do any of the other 24,999 people realize they are part of this group?" I queried mentally.

"Subconsciously they know, but we are informing you so you can inform them. No one else in the group is in a better position to assist them in opening to this awareness."

"For what purpose?"

"Each of the 25,000 is supporting the shared goal in his own way. You write books and offer seminars. So do a few of the others. Some are helping to integrate the ideas into business, music, movies, and mass communications. Many are taking the ideas into medicine and health care. Others simply read the books and share the ideas with friends. But, in his own way, each is contributing by his involvement. Once fully aware of their purpose, each will intensify his efforts."

While making notes about these inner communications, I recalled my visions of Teotihuacan. "Ever since my visit to Teotihuacan, I've had occasional flashes of being on top of one of the pyramids at night, surrounded by others wearing white robes. I'm holding a long crystal rod pulsating with blue light that appears to be keeping a mob of angry people back. What is all that about?"

"You will discover the answer yourself as you begin to explore this subject anew. You have refined your skills since you first encountered your destiny in Mexico. It is time to open the doors again."

"Why is this so important?"

"The ideas you love so much transcend spirituality. They are very powerful and they can be used either to serve or to enslave. You know this. You feel this. You think about it often. As your group continues to attain success, what happened in Teotihuacan is likely to happen again. If the awareness is misused, it will eventually be banned by those who will revolt against it. History will repeat itself."

"So tell me what really happened in Teotihuacan," I said as quietly as possible, so as not to awaken Tara.

"No, it will be much more meaningful for you to rediscover your history with those who shared it with you. The gathering continues. You will know what to do. You can go back to sleep now."

A month later, while conducting a seven-day seminar in Palm Springs, California, I decided to do a Teotihuacan past-life regression with the group of 250 participants. A brief explanation of my experiences served as introduction. The already well-conditioned participants prepared for the session by breathing deeply as they watched large-screen video-hypnosis images combined with my verbal preparation and induction. I told the participants: "If you are indeed one of a large group of people who once lived in Teotihuacan, and you have reincarnated as part of a group pact to share New Age ideas, you are now going to go back in time and relive some of your experiences as part of that civilization."

I directed the group to explore many specific aspects of that lifetime. After awakening them, I asked, "How many of you feel you were part of what happened in Teotihuacan?"

Approximately two-thirds of the hands went up—about 150 to 175 people. Many were upset by the experience. Some volunteered to share what they had observed in regression. As they did, goose bumps ran up and down my arms; they were describing the things I had seen myself in visions and regressions.

I conducted the Teotihuacan regression again in Sedona, Denver, Philadelphia, and Los Angeles. In each city the results were the same. At least two-thirds of those present shared the Teotihuacan experience, and the stories supported each other.

A critic argued that it was group suggestion. Naturally, that's a possibility, but I've had too many similar experiences with groups to agree. When Ruth Montgomery first began to write about "walk-ins," I decided to do some experimental regressions to see how many seminar participants were walk-ins. Just about everyone wanted to be, but in a group of two or three hundred, only a couple of people would perceive impressions, a percentage that statistically supported Ruth's communications about the number of souls crossing over in this manner.

In the summer/fall of 1987 we set out on a twenty-one-city tour, traveling from coast to coast and back again in a big, black Silver Eagle entertainers' bus. The tour started July 31 in Sedona and ended October 12 back in Los Angeles. The Eagle had been used by many of the biggest rock bands in the country. There was a living room, kitchen, and entertainment center in front, twelve bunks and a bathroom in the middle, and a bedroom in the back with a double bed for Tara and me and a small crib for Hunter. "There are real carnal vibes back here," Tara said upon entering the bedroom for the first time.

"Very inspiring," I said.

"I noticed," she said.

After a month on the road she was pregnant again.

"It's a bus baby," she said.

"It was the carnal vibes," I said.

CHAPTER SEVEN

California
1987

Don Tinling was one of sixty people attending my five-day Professional Hypnotist Training in the seminar center of our offices in Agoura Hills, California, back in October 1987. Don had long black hair, and usually dressed in black as well. He was always a few minutes late for the morning session, but he paid strict attention to the communications. The female participants, drawn by his good looks and friendly manner, were quick to choose him as a partner for the exercises and practice sessions.

His seminar sign-up sheet explained that he was a twenty-five-year-old New York City actor who worked informally as a New Age counselor. He was attending the seminar to refine his skills as a past-life therapist.

As soon as I met Don, I "knew" him. I meet thousands of people every year, but this experience of affinity happens very rarely. The first substantiation of an ancient bond came when I decided to conduct a group Teotihuacan past-life regression as a demonstration. All sixty trainees participated.

After the regression, three of the participants were outwardly upset by their experiences. During the bathroom break, I talked to the first two. The third one was Don. He stood on the outside balcony, his head down.

"Would you like to talk about it, or would you rather have some space for a while?" I asked.

"I'd like to talk about it," he replied, obviously still quite upset. "I was an alien to the earth who assumed human form, or 'walked into' a human body. I know that sounds weird, but it was one of the most vivid experiences I've ever had."

"You may be weird, but at least you're not alone," I said. "This is the fifth time I've conducted this regression, and in the previous sessions many of the subjects have told me about aliens or spaceships. If there is anything I'm not personally interested in, it's aliens and spaceships, but I can't ignore their experiences."

Don continued to describe his past-life regression. "I was an alien, but we were all a part of the same higher consciousness or divine force, and it was time to join forces."

Many of Don's details related to information I had previously received myself or heard from others. One area we all agreed on was clothing: "We wore robes or tunics with colored ribbing around the edges, about one and a half inches from the hem and three inches wide. Everyone dressed in variations on the same style."

When Don mentioned the information and knowledge-storage system he had worked with, I felt myself shiver. "They were almost like bricks. Solid, yet made up of different segments of glass. They were like thick stained-glass windows held together without leading."

I had seen exactly the same thing in my own visions and regressions, many months before. I hadn't told anyone, not even Tara, because it didn't seem important at the time. The colored crystals were in a secret storage room known only to a small inner council. It was in this room that we preserved the knowledge and planned our strategies. I already knew that Tara and I had been part of the council. Evidently, Don had been ttoo.

Excitedly, we shared more information during the seminar and in the weeks that followed, over the phone and through the mail. That Christmas he came to California, spent some of the holidays with our family, and began to talk about moving to Los Angeles. Tara and I encouraged him to do it.

One of Don's regressive experiences seemed to bother him because it was so improbable. The following is from his notes:

I was standing beside a young girl who I perceived to be my daughter. I was a man, but this is quite limiting in describing myself. I was taller than most of the others, almost a different species. My daughter seemed to be like everyone else. She had long, shiny dark hair with bangs, and big black eyes. When I realized she was my daughter, I began to search for her mother. Then, it was as if I could "see" the organs inside my body. They weren't human. I realized I was capable of reproduction. I had given birth to this girl with human form. It was as if there was some sort of embryo inside of me that was capable of binary fission.

My intention was to have a child who could survive whatever was to become of this civilization. She would be able to pass along everything she learned to future generations—the knowledge existing in her memory banks that could later, somehow, be transferred to others.

In searching the Edgar Cayce records, I found the following reading that seemed to relate to what Don had experienced:

Reading 2390–1; Nov. 2, 1940: The sleeping prophet discussed the past life of an individual who had lived ". . . in Atlantean land during period of changing of individuals from double sex or the abilities of progeneration of activities of self."

Atlantis predated Teotihuacan, but I was beginning to accept that Teotihuacan was an historical extension of Atlantis.

Reading 5750–1; Nov. 12, 1933: "That which we find would be of particular interest would be that which superseded the Aztec civilization. In that preceding this we had rather a combination of sources, or as high civilization that was influenced by injection of forces from other channels, other sources . . ."

I wondered if "injection of forces from other channels" could mean aliens from other worlds who arrived in Teotihuacan in space ships. I remembered my 1974 visit to the ruins of the once great city and the raised platforms in the Citadel.

Fifty or sixty seminar participants had by now sent me transcripts of their Teotihuacan past-life experience as one of the group of 25,000. Many mentioned space ships.

"It's just getting too damned weird for me," I told Tara.

"That's only because of the UFO and binary fission stuff, Richard. Don't get stuck on that when there's so much about Teotihuacan that you know relates to our past," she said.

"Maybe."

"Besides, snails can function as either males or females, giving or receiving sperm. So why not humans?"

"Snails can do that?"

Tara nodded. I walked over to the bookshelf and scanned our reference books. "Surprisingly, sea slugs [snails] have reached a state of sexual development far beyond that of Homo sapiens, since they are simultaneous hermaphrodites," said one source. It went on to describe the mating habits of sea slugs, explaining that they engaged in precoital foreplay and delighted in group sexual orgies. There was a lot more, but I didn't read it.

"I think Madame Blavatsky and some other Theosophical Society writers talked about it too," Tara said.

"Blavatsky? Really?"

My wife's near photographic memory always amazes me. I found my copies of *The Secret Doctrine;* three volumes, 1300 pages, published in 1888. Madame Helena Petrovna Blavatsky was a Russian mystic and adventurer who, after traveling in India and Tibet, claimed that she had been initiated by Masters into the secrets of esoteric mysticism. She founded the Theosophical Society in 1875. Her Masters helped her write the books that became the foundation of modern theosophy—one of the primary sources for our generally accepted metaphysical concepts. I'd never read more than a few sections of her esoteric, archaically worded books, but in the index to *The Secret Doctrine* there were numerous references to hermaphrodites and androgynes.

"When have you had the time to study this?" I asked Tara as I flipped to the references.

"I just read the abridgement," she said with a wide smile, pointing to a thin volume in the bookcase.

Blavatsky claimed that the Lemurian people of the third root race were extremely tall hermaphrodites. "The one became two," she said. Over the centuries they evolved into a bisexual or androgynous people, and eventually into distinct males and females.

"Aren't there often two root races living at the same time, overlapping each other? And didn't the Lemurians and Atlanteans interact?" Tara asked.

"Sure. The Lemurians were supposed to be the third root race, the Atlanteans the fourth, and we're the fifth."

"And aren't you convinced that Atlanteans colonized Egypt, Central America, and Mexico? That Teotihuacan was directly influenced by the Atlantean civilization?"

"Agreed. So based on this generally accepted esoteric awareness, it's logical that Don could have had his own kid. But that still leaves the UFOs."

Tara laughed. "It's really the UFOs, isn't it? You really have a problem with UFOs."

"I've managed to avoid writing about or in any way relating to UFOs since I got into this business," I said. "They always used to come up in Atlantis regressions. It's not that I don't accept the possibility of their existence—the subject just turns me off."

"If you decide to write a book on Teotihuacan and the 25,000, I think you're going to have to stretch," Tara said, and smiled her all-knowing smile. "Maybe you'll just have to play the newspaper reporter on this one."

I nodded.

"Maybe space aliens will turn out to be part of the story? Then what?"

"I can't relate to that."

"You don't relate too well to crystals either. They also seem to be part of the story."

"Uh-huh."

"I think sometimes you fool yourself about who you are."

I listened.

"You don't really relate to what the New Age movement has become. You're considered one of the leaders because you've written best-selling books on reincarnation, because of your seminars and the impact of your magazine. You know the New Age inside and out. You write about it. You incorporate some of the ideas into your life, but overall it isn't you. Often, you find it an embarrassment. You tell people you're Zen-based, but that isn't quite true either, because you have no interest in the meditative side of Zen," Tara said.

"Zen incorporates karma and reincarnation, and the other ideas I treasure: conscious detachment, the acceptance of what is, the power of the mind, self-responsibility, and so on," I said.

"Right, all the aspects of Zen historically accepted by the Samurai," she said, and paused. "By the warrior class. Your introduction to this kind of thinking came through your involvement in Chinese martial arts, remember?"

Remember? Always! In the late sixties I spent a lot of time in a Phoenix river-bottom karate dojo. My sensei was stern, detached, and unpredictable. He had been part of an experimental army project to train twelve men to kill instinctively—if something moved in the shadows, kill it. No consideration for right or wrong. Just kill. Of the original twelve, Sensei thought he was the only one still alive. The others died in action or could not be deprogrammed; some were killed by police.

We bowed to Sensei upon entering the dojo, barefooted in our white *gis*—afraid, but in a way that brought out the best in us. He taught the Kenpo system, but he was a man always reminding himself not to kill, so the specter of death oozed out into his words and demonstrations. When he learned I was frequenting Waylon Jennings's nightclub, J.D.'s, across the street, he tailored my private lessons to fit the situation.

"J.D.'s is a fight waiting to happen. If a man is drunk or stoned, it will take him twenty seconds to feel pain. Do you know what a man can do to you in twenty seconds, Sutphen?"

When I didn't answer, he told me.

"He can hurt you, maim you, kill you. *You never give him that chance.*" Then he would teach me how to break bones and incapacitate the inebriated. He took particular pleasure in demonstrating how to strike a devastating blow in a crowd of people so that no one but your target noticed what you'd done.

After intense group-sparring sessions, we students would sit on the floor and Sensei would become philosophical. "The strong are patient," he would say over and over, like a mantra. "If you are physically endangered, react instantly. But in all other situations in life, resist your inclination to immediately react to external circumstances. The goal is to keep your mind like calm water, so that it accurately reflects everything within striking range. Anger only clouds the water and assures defeat. Pause. Allow the water to calm. Consider the alternatives and potential results. Then act with clear intention and total commitment."

I adopted the logical Zen philosophy. The more I studied, the more I wanted to know. Exploring the concepts of reincarnation and karma opened a doorway to the entire metaphysical world. At that time there were hundreds of metaphysical organizations in the Phoenix valley. Most of those that I investigated turned me off, but I couldn't deny some personal experiences that kept me interested and involved.

"Dojo Zen doesn't relate much to white light, UFOs, crystal power, or the Harmonic Convergence," Tara said, bringing me back to the present.

I couldn't help laughing. My wife was right. Thousands claimed the Harmonic Convergence was a turning point in their lives. It certainly was in mine. To me and most of those close to me the whole thing was a clear case of word-of-mouth, cosmic foo-foo marketing that made the New Age the laughingstock of the media, from the comic strip Doonesbury to *Time* magazine. When it was over, I began to distance myself more than ever from the emerging image of the New Age movement, refocusing my energy and seminar communications on the Bushido ideals that had always formed the philosophical basis of my reality.

"Most New Agers are very unrealistic," I said.

"They're visionaries. You're a pragmatist," she said. "Make it all right with yourself to be an objective reporter on Teotihuacan. If Don or twenty-three percent of the respondents perceive space ships in their regressions, just report the figures and let your readers draw their own conclusions. Look at Jess Stearn—he's made a career out of being an objective metaphysical reporter."

"Space ships?" I said.

"Space ships," she said. "With some crystals thrown in."

"Does pregnancy make you so wise?" I asked.

"Of course," she said.

Cheyenne Tara Sutphen was born April 27, 1988. With black hair and big blue eyes, she was a miniature version of her mother.

CHAPTER EIGHT

California
1988

By the spring of 1988 seminar participants had sent me enough Teotihuacan case histories to fill two thick file folders. Tara had hypnotized and directed me through several Teotihuacan past-life regressions. I read everything I could find on the archeological history of the city, and discovered that even some old Edgar Cayce readings cast some light on the overall picture of what happened 1400 years ago.

I decided to seriously pursue a Teotihuacan psychic investigation. One of the first steps was to develop a set of prerecorded past-life regression tapes titled *Teotihuacan*. The two-tape album was beautifully packaged and contained four thirty-minute programs:

(1) Teotihuacan: Background & Preparation
(2) Teotihuacan General Past-Life Regression
(3) Teotihuacan Suppression Period Past-Life Regression
(4) Teotihuacan Conflict Regression

We added the album to our Valley of the Sun line, and it was soon distributed to hundreds of retail outlets. On the back of the album I explained that it was part of an ongoing research study, and I invited anyone who used it successfully to send me their story, along with permission to reprint it. In return I would add them to a special list of people to be informed of new information we received on Teotihuacan as it was uncovered.

Master of Life is a quarterly Valley of the Sun magazine/catalog we send free to approximately 150,000 recent seminar participants and book/tape buyers, and to at least 100,000 new names supplied for each mailing by list brokers. In the April 1988 issue we offered the tape album for sale and published the first of a two-part story about the Teotihuacan experience. Soon the case histories were pouring into the office.

In May my editor from Pocket Books was in Los Angeles for the American Booksellers Association convention. We met at my home in Malibu to discuss the new book I was writing, *Finding Your Answers Within*. The book, my fifth for Pocket, had been her idea. She'd told me they wanted to publish a manual on New Age self-exploration techniques, and asked if I was interested. I knew it would be an easy book to write, and agreed to take on the project. The final manuscript was due in August.

The book was proceeding well, but my disenchantment with much of the New Age movement wasn't helping me generate the needed energy. When considering a new project or direction, I always ask myself and others, "Do you really have the energy for it?" If you do, and if you are clear about your intent, the battle is already half won. But if you don't have the energy, your chances of winning are slim. You'll soon lose interest and put the project behind you, usually sacrificing some self-esteem in the process. When Tara had encouraged me to write another book for Pocket Books, my first reaction was, "I just don't think I have the energy to create another successful mass-market metaphysical title." My first books for Pocket were filled with the enthusiasm of discovery—that's what made them so successful. You can't fake that. A reader always senses an author's sincerity and energy.

But Tara's ideas are very important to me, and I continued to think about the possibility until I remembered some of the advice I share with seminar participants: "Don't assume there is only one way to attain your goals." So I asked myself, "What aspect of metaphysical investigation is most exciting to me?" The answer was easy, and hadn't changed since I'd written *You Were Born Again to Be Together* fourteen years earlier: romantic relationships, and the idea of love spanning several lifetimes.

"What would really challenge you in regard to your work?" I asked myself next. "To stretch my abilities as a writer"—another easy answer. That did it. I'd identified a completely new challenge, and I'd found my energy. I had collected some wonderful, well-documented case histories over the years, and I decided to try to write about them in a totally different way—in "third-person limited." Could I communicate those true stories in a fast-paced, short-story format, like a television docudrama? Could I incorporate my Zen/metaphysical philosophy without slowing down the action? I feel *Predestined Love* proved that the answer to both questions was yes.

I didn't feel this kind of energy or challenge when I was working on *Finding Your Answers Within,* but the idea of creating a textbook that would read quickly and deliver life-changing information offered enough excitement to keep the words flowing. My agent seemed pleased with my progress, and I gave her copies of the completed pages. During our meeting I also mentioned the ongoing Teotihuacan investigation and the possibility of writing a book on the subject. She liked the idea and wanted to see a proposal when *Answers* was completed.

The Twelfth Annual Seven-Day Transcendence Training was held in Palm Springs, California, June 19–25, 1988. Three hundred people attended, representing most of the fifty states. The theme was "The Wisdom to Transform Consciousness," and as in preceding years, I invited some author friends to be guest speakers. The 1988 list included Jess Stearn, author of *The Sleeping Prophet,* whose latest book, *Soulmates,* was still generating a lot of interest; Jach Pursel, who channels Lazaris and had just published *The Sacred Journey;* and Dr. Edith Fiore, who shared information from her new book, *The Unquiet Dead.* Also participating were Alan Vaughan, *Pattern of Prophecy;* D. Scott Rogo, *Parapsychology: A Century of Inquiry;* Bob Trask, *God's Phone Number;* and Eileen Connolly, *Tarot—New Handbook for the Apprentice;* along with many less well-known practitioners. Several singers and musician friends dropped in during the week to promote their new albums and entertain the group. We scheduled four sessions a day and I conducted Bushido human-potential sessions for three hours each morning.

Don Tinling, now living in California, where he had established a regression/counseling practice, was backing me up by conducting evening sessions at my Sedona Psychic Seminars. At the Transcendence Training, he was to follow Jess Stearn's Tuesday-afternoon talk on reincarnation with a group past-life regression. At the last minute I asked Don if he would also fill in for the Tuesday-evening speaker, who had been forced to cancel at the last minute. He agreed.

Over the dinner break Don felt the need to meditate on the content of the evening sessions. He aligned his crystals and precious stones around him and went into a deep, altered state of consciousness.

"It was a very powerful meditation," Don said later. "I was told to conduct a general past-life regression and then, before the mid-session bathroom break, to announce that I might do a Teotihuacan regression after the break. I think I was in contact with my guides. They said the Teotihuacan regression should not be experienced by everyone. So, when I came out of the trance, I decided to conduct the session if a good percentage of the participants did not come back after the break."

"Did a lot of them leave?" I asked.

"Yes, so I conducted the regression. I didn't have a script. I think I channeled it," he said.

"What was the result?"

"Intense. I've never had an audience react like that. As you know, it doesn't leave you uplifted and inspired. They were emotionally moved by the power of the experience and they wanted to know why. They were confused the same way I was. The same way you were after your Mexican experience."

Weeks later, on a Saturday afternoon, Tara and I were sitting in Don's apartment in the hills above Hollywood. He showed us the large stack of Teotihuacan mail he had received in response to the session.

"Why don't you write the story?" I suggested.

"I'd be glad to give it a try, but if you write it, the book will have a large audience waiting for it to be published," he said. "Do you think you have the energy for it?" He smiled at using my own processing techniques on me.

"I don't know yet, but I won't start it unless I do."

"He'll do it, but not for the reasons you think," Tara said.

Don and I looked at her. I didn't have the faintest idea what she was getting at.

"Some of our antagonists in Teotihuacan have reincarnated as leaders of the fundamentalist religious right. Richard knows that now," Tara said. "Once again, our liberating ideas are being pitted against their restrictive attempts to control society. It's a battle Richard can't pass up. He'll have enough energy for six people."

"Chrissake!" I said. Tara and Don laughed. I walked out on Don's deck and gazed across the smog-shrouded city. In the distance the tall buildings of Century City rose up out of the ochre haze. Los Angeles loomed off to my left. I thought about how much I liked this city and how much I disliked the zealots who were trying to drive us back to the dark ages of religious intolerance. For four years Tara and I had worked with the American Civil Liberties Union (ACLU), People for the American Way, and our own nonprofit organization to fight them in court and on the propaganda front.

As a result, several born-again Christian authors had condemned me in their books, just as they had condemned people like Norman Lear, Marilyn Ferguson, and Buckminster Fuller. I was in good company.

Now, Ronald Reagan was about to leave office. Jimmy Swaggart, Tammy and Jim Bakker, and other fundamentalist leaders had orchestrated their own downfall. Pat Robertson wasn't even carrying the southern states in the election primaries. The IRS was investigating the whole movement, and there were rumors that Jerry Falwell's Moral Majority might be folding. Most of the religious right's legislation to restrict metaphysical practitioners had been blocked. On the surface, it appeared that reason was winning, but I knew that true believers never give up. I also knew I'd write the book on Teotihuacan and the 25,000.

CHAPTER NINE

California
1989

Ruth Montgomery's writing style and the fascinating stories she tells have always captivated me. I consider Ruth a friend; we keep in touch with postcards and letters and we've led seminars together. She has provided me with personal messages from her guides and wrote a chapter about me in one of her books.

"You respect Ruth Montgomery's work, don't you, Richard?" Tara asked, sitting down across from me in my writing studio. My wife was now helping me research the Teotihuacan story.

"Of course," I said.

"If you read this book when it came out, you read it thirteen years ago." She held up a copy of Ruth's best-seller, *The World Before.*

"Right."

"Well, as you say, what you resist, you draw to you. Ruth channeled this from her guides, and it's about crystals and spaceships."

"Read on," I said, and laughed.

"This is from a chapter titled 'Airships of Antiquity,'" Tara noted, and began to read:

89

"Visiting space people told Atlanteans how to prepare the giant crystals after they had already begun to harness energy with smaller crystals that operated labor-saving devices. From a hillside on Atlantis they found a vein of quartz sufficient in size to reflect all rays of the sun and moon, for the moon had its part to play in this tremendous experiment. By cutting away the earth from all sides, they then etched facets so delicate as to reflect every ray, and since there was nothing in the atmosphere in those pristine days to deflect the sun's rays, they had constant use of the Crystal except during occasional rains. By producing more energy than essential to each day's usage, they found a way to store the energy in copper vats so that no plane or ship depended on one day's energy supply to propel it on proper course."

Tara looked at me over the top of the book to see if she had my attention. She did.

"Listen to what it says a couple of paragraphs later," she said.

"These space visitors arrived in airships of remarkable design thought-into-being by highly advanced minds in the spirit plane, for until they reached the earth's atmosphere they had no need of machinery, and earth time is nonexistent beyond our atmosphere. Then they would produce the electrical components out of earth products that had been turned into gaseous elements. It sounds farfetched, but the records are here to prove it.

"With these machines as a prototype, the Atlanteans quickly put together similar craft composed of solids capable of being propelled by energy from the Crystal in all directions, depending on the facets left uncovered for a particular journey. Some who worked on the inventions were souls who had previously been in the earth plane as shadow-like forms and well understood the power of the mind. Others followed their patterns and soon demonstrated that the will is more powerful than the idea, for it is easier to invent something if you know in advance that it will work. Seeing machines brought to earth by outer-space beings proved the workability, and all doubt was therefore removed. It is so even today. When one nation discovers atomic power and demonstrates its practical application, it is less difficult for another nation to produce it, knowing that it is a workable project."

[Ruth's guides continued:] "Spacemen landed on Atlantis in such numbers as to prove that man would be able to fly with a proper understanding of aerodynamics. They came in planes of varying pattern, but most had discs and whirling engines to defy the law of gravity both in take-off and landing."

I showed Tara the book I was reading, *The Story of Atlantis* by W. Scott-Elliot. Written in 1896, some of the content was channeled via what the author called "astral clairvoyance."

"Listen to a few of the items I've highlighted," I said, and began to read.

"The Popul Vuh *(one of only five pre-Columbian books the Spanish priests did not destroy)* speaks of a visit paid by three sons of the King of the Quiches *(Mayans)* to a land in the east of the shores of the sea whence their fathers had come, from which they brought back among other things *a system of writing* [emphasis added].

"Scott-Elliot claims Atlantis submerged following earthquakes in 9564 B.C.," I said. "Here's something else that's interesting. At the time of Teotihuacan in central Mexico, Mayan cities flourished on the Yucatan Peninsula and in Guatemala. The following is a translation of Mayan writings that can be seen in the British Museum. It's said to relate to the home of their ancestors and the final catastrophe of the Atlantean island of Poseidon.

"In the year six Kan, on the eleventh Muluc in the month Zac, there occurred terrible earthquakes which continued without interruption until the thirteenth Chuen. The country of the hills of mud, the land of Mu, was sacrificed: being twice upheaved, it suddenly disappeared during the night, the basin being continually shaken by volcanic forces. Being confined, these caused the land to sink and to rise several times and in various places. At last the surface gave way and ten countries were torn asunder and scattered. Unable to stand the force of the convulsions, they sank with their 64,000,000 inhabitants 8060 years before the writing of this book."

I paused for a deep breath. "Here's another interesting item. The author claims, 'wheat was not evolved on this planet at all. It was the gift of the Manu, who brought it from another globe outside our chain of worlds. But oats and some other cereals are the result of crosses between wheat and the indigenous grasses of the earth. Now the experiments which gave these results were carried out in the agricultural schools of Atlantis.'"

Atlantis was a familiar subject to me. Twenty-three well-read books on the legendary island continent sat in my bookcase. For sixteen years I'd directed Atlantis past-life regressions with individuals, with small groups and with thousands of people in my seminars. Back in the early seventies, in Scottsdale, Arizona, I had learned to do group regressions. Three grade-school teachers asked me to regress their classes, and when I did, not a single parent complained. Doing that today would probably prompt a front-page story in the local paper.

On different occasions I had regressed a sixth-, seventh- and eighth-grade class back to a lifetime on Atlantis. I told the children nothing about the lost civilization, but when the session was over and my subjects awakened, they were quick to tell me about the widespread use of crystals, the gleaming cities, tunic-style attire, sound chambers, and other things I already knew from my own experience, reading, psychic investigations, and regressions with adults.

Refreshing my memory regarding the Atlantis "mother country" was the next step in my investigation of Teotihuacan. *The Shadow of Atlantis* by Colonel A. Braghine examines the archeological, anthropological, historical, and scientific evidence that indicates a number of pre-Columbian civilizations were established by Atlanteans.

According to Edgar Cayce's readings, this migration took place over a twelve-thousand-year period, from 28,000 B.C. until the final destruction. Cayce points out that people from the continent of Lemuria, in the Pacific, also migrated to Mexico and Central America.

The following Edgar Cayce readings support the idea of a migration and the use of aircraft:

Reading 1710–3; April 12, 1939: ". . . in Atlantis when there was the breaking up of the land, came to what was called the Mayan land, or what is now Yucatan—entity was the first to cross the water in the plane or air machine of that period."

Reading 1599–1; May 28, 1938: ". . . in the Atlantean land during those periods when there were the activities that brought about the last destruction through the warring of Sons of the Law of One and Sons of Belial—among those sent to what later became the Yucatan land of the Mayan experiences."

Reading 3611–1; Dec. 31, 1943: ". . . in Atlantean land when there were those periods of the last upheavals or the disappearance of the isles of Posedia. [The entity was] among those who went to what later became known as the Inca land—the Peruvian land as called in the present."

Most of the books on Atlantis quote Plato, and provide convincing evidence that the lost continent once existed, was populated by a highly advanced civilization that lasted for thousands of years, and colonized much of the world. I'm not going to take the space to duplicate that information here. Instead I'll share my awareness of Atlantis as it existed before the final cataclysm, approximately ten thousand years ago. This information is based on my past-life regressions with others and on my psychic investigations and studies. Naturally, any civilization that endured for thousands of years underwent extensive changes in regard to all aspects of life: governmental structure, scientific development, lifestyle, sexuality, diet, dress, and spiritual beliefs. Just look at how our own country has been transformed in only two hundred years! This is why people regressed to a lifetime on Atlantis often come back with widely divergent stories of what they experienced there.

THE ATLANTEAN CIVILIZATION

Atlantean society in its most evolved form allowed freedom of expression and purpose, and encouraged those belonging to the upper castes to become all they were capable of being. The island continent was populated by people of different races and colors, but the majority of Atlanteans had black hair and a skin color like that of the American Indians. Women were considered equal to men, but during periods when they outnumbered men, polygamy was encouraged and men could lawfully marry two wives.

Marriage was supposed to be based on vibrational compatibility, and the ceremony was performed by a temple priest or priestess. If the relationship didn't work, the union was dissolved by the temple authorities without any unpleasantness. Those who did not want to marry were encouraged to have lovers and out-of-wedlock children, if both parents were good mental and physical specimens. A large number of women worked as surrogate mothers in state-run child-rearing centers.

Many young people were drafted to serve the greater good of the society in a capacity best suited to their talents. This often meant being assigned to a specific technical school, which left the individual no choice as to his life work.

The country was ruled by an emperor and divided into provinces managed by appointed viceroys. The viceroys were responsible for governing their own province and for ensuring the well-being of the people. This included overseeing agricultural development. Harvested crops were distributed equally among the people of the province.

At the bottom of the Atlantean caste system were the mutants, or "things," described by Edgar Cayce, Ruth Montgomery, and many others. These were life-form experiments that had failed, trapping entities in hideous bodies—some half man, half animal, others human but with gruesome appendages. The mutants labored as slaves, often on farms. Next came the common laborers, production workers, and servants. Technical workers, artisans, and researchers stood one rung higher, and at the top of the system were seven levels of elders and priests, just beneath the viceroys and emperor. The color of the belt each priest wore around his waist indicated his level of awareness.

Upper-class women wore tunics, or short or long gowns. Men dressed in tunics, kilts, and sandals. Their clothing was usually white or a very light pastel.

Psychic abilities were highly respected and encouraged, especially among the upper classes. Those who were naturally empathic and developed their gift, ranked high in the caste system. Psychic development was taught in the schools, and there was a time when everyone was connected psychically. But when the mind-link began to be misused for selfish purposes, the people "disconnected." After this mental bond was severed, one regression subject reported sorrowfully, "It's so lonely now."

Crystals played an important part in Atlantean life and were used primarily to heal and to project the power of the mind. The Atlanteans beamed light through crystals, transmitting different healing rays to regenerate tissue and organs. Vibrational sound chambers were also used as part of the physical and/or mental healing process. At the age of ten children studied the subtleties of vibrational sound in their schools.

The Atlanteans believed in an all-powerful Supreme

Being, symbolized by the sun (or a circle). They considered their god so omnipotent that his name could not be mentioned, except as an O sound that was hummed as "Ohm."

This, then, was the heritage of the people who founded Teotihuacan thousands of years later.

SECTION

II

Letters and Information

CHAPTER TEN

Letters

Of the hundreds of letters I received about Teotihuacan, many verified my past-life regression experiences as well as Tara's, or helped us to understand life in those ancient times. The following excerpts illustrate the range of emotions generated by memories of Teotihuacan:

Carol A. Reiners, San Francisco: "I really wish you had never mentioned Teotihuacan. Since I read the story in your magazine I have been having horrible nightmares."

Jolene Duff, Wilmer, Alaska: "I received *Master of Life* Issue 37 today and am in an absolute state of shock as a result of your article, 'Reincarnation of the 25,000.' I've never written before but am compelled to do so now. Before going further, I want you to know that I am a forty-year-old rational woman not given to illusions or nonsense. My IQ ranges in the top two percent of the nation and I am very logically oriented.

"I did not begin reading your article with any expectations, the title meant nothing to me, the word 'Teotihuacan' meant nothing to me—it was just another interesting subject, like so many others I've read in your magazine over the years. However, when I read the pronounciation, 'Teh-oh-tee-wah-kahn,' I nearly passed out. I'm still so emotionally shaken I can hardly compose this letter. You see, that word, that pronunciation, is very familiar to me; I've been living with its sound reverberating through my mind for the past six years."

Jolene goes on to describe a spontaneous vision she experienced on more than one occasion while living in Houston, Texas.

"I saw a young man with long dark hair and dark skin rising to a full stance from inside a small doorway. He is bare-chested and wears something in his hair and something around his neck. Before I can identify the objects, his dark eyes catch me and he looks right through my soul. I can't breathe and the name Teotihuacan echoes and echoes through my mind. My heart aches and I feel an unbelievable yearning. It's indescribable, a bittersweet feeling of pain and love.

"These flashes or visions went on for weeks throughout the days and woke me during the nights. I couldn't think about anything else, and searched everywhere for some kind of clue as to what the word Teotihuacan meant. Then one day I had a different vision in which a man came to me in a white robe. He had a ruddy complexion and the kindest face you could imagine. He introduced himself and said he had come to give me information. I told him I wouldn't be able to remember it, but he smiled and reassured me.

"He took my hands and began speaking very slowly, but as he went along, he would speed up until I became so frantic I stopped him in exasperation. I begged him to slow down. My brain was throbbing with the content and speed of it. I could not understand the technical words. He said, 'It's not important that you understand now. When the time comes, if it comes, you will know what to do.'

"That was the last of the visions. I still don't understand, and I am eager to learn more about this."

Zola Simmons, Medford, Oregon: "In 1973 I visited Teotihuacan with my husband. The ancient city did not impress him greatly, but it simply turned me inside out. I walked the Avenue of the Dead and a tremendous wave of sadness engulfed me and I started weeping inside like a lost child. By evening I announced that I had to stay overnight and be there at sunrise. I slept little. The next morning I climbed to the top of the pyramid. The sun cast its pink glow over all, a soft breeze gently blew, then suddenly, from the full length of the avenue, I could hear the wailing and lament and confusion of thousands of people. There is no way to really describe their terror. I stayed at the top of the pyramid several hours. It was a psychic experience beyond description, and I have had many."

Joseph R. Lucas, MSc.D., Lubbock, Texas: "My recent Teotihuacan regressions in your Palm Springs and Albuquerque seminars were so vivid, and kept 'flashing back' in the days and weeks following the seminars, that last month I decided that I would have to go to Teotihuacan.

"So I did. While visiting that Sacred Place, I experienced a gradual feeling of deep depression, which grew to such intensity that after about an hour of exploration, I said, 'I've simply got to get out of here!' And we left."

The following are excerpts from letters describing past-life regression experiences that occurred in the seminars or when working with the prerecorded tapes. Each excerpt is included not because it is unique, but because it is representative of so many others.

Paula Muldare, Chicago: "I saw myself as a religious healer who used my hands to restore positive energy.

First, a jolly old man, bent and crippled, got onto a table. I moved my hands over his whole body and sent the energy into him. Then a little girl came skipping up to the table and I repeated the same thing. There seemed to be a line of people waiting for me to work on them."

In her fifteen-page letter, she explained that today she is an activist fighting for handicapped children's rights. Paula also described another kind of mind power:

"I was spotted by soldiers and they began to chase me, so I projected my thoughts ahead and found a small, low badger cave in the hill. I hid in the cave and sent the animal in it calming thoughts until the soldiers had passed."

Karen E. Smith, Raceland, Kentucky: "I realized I was male, a craftsman who fashioned temple adornments and utensils from obsidian. I was young, about thirty-five years old, with a nice home in an apartment complex not far from the Temple of the Sun. I felt very proud because my work was highly valued. I had two wives and six sons and was very happy in this lifetime."

Later Karen explains, "I saw five ships come out of the sky. They were like glowing disks, shining so brightly that I could not look directly at them. The men who emerged from the ships were humanlike, but they seemed to glow, so that you couldn't tell where their bodies ended and the light began."

Mary L. Ayala, Houston: "My father was at least seven feet tall. And he was huge. He seemed to project a light, so that it was hard to look at him for very long. He was quite blond, with curly hair and beard. His eyes were light blue and seemed to pierce every object he looked upon. He was outlandishly dressed, holding a conical gold helmet that reminded me of a bird cage. He wore a fire-red tunic with gold chest armor, and knee-high gold boots. He was not from the planet earth, but came from another place in the planetary system and chose my mother as his mate."

Mary provides nine pages of information and explains that there were many races living in Teotihuacan, including Negroid people. The many races were mentioned in several letters.

Lee Burritt, Camillus, New York: Lee was one of two dozen people who emphasized that the wisdom of the time was programmed into crystals—that the books I sought were actually crystals. I found this hard to accept until another reader wrote to tell me about a report they'd just seen on CNN. It seems that science has now discovered that crystal blocks are capable of storing 25,000 megabytes of information.

Lee says, "The crystal had many uses: storing knowledge, imparting special energy, and creating harmony and healing. Some crystals were used to project the will of the owner. Near the end, we recorded all the remaining wisdom into the crystals. Those of us who were to leave did so via underground tunnels that connected the temples with the interior of a huge extinct volcano. Other tunnels led from the volcano to a distance outside the city. We carried as many of the crystals as possible, dividing them among several groups, leaving at intervals over a lengthy period."

With the exception of the clover-leaf rooms we'd visited below the Pyramid of the Sun, I knew nothing about any tunnels beneath Teotihuacan. But after several days of research we found a report that claimed two hundred major volcanic caves have been discovered in the area. Only three have been explored, and it's now known that these caves and tunnels were used as a sanctuary for religious devotees even before Teotihuacan came into being. One of the caves lies directly under the Pyramid of the Sun (beneath the clover-leaf rooms), and according to research supervisor Ruben Cabrera in a report filed with the Mexico City News, "Studies conclude that inhabitants decided to construct the Pyramid of the Sun over the cave because they considered the cave a source of magic."

Sandra L. Smith, Palmetto, Florida: "In the regression, I learned that I was a digger of tunnels, who stayed in the tunnels and knew no other life. It was very frightening and I felt oppressed. On my fourth attempt with the tapes, I experienced the tunnel collapse and bury me alive. I can't put on paper the feeling that is still with me of the dirt crashing down and being unable to breathe."

Alice Bryant, Alto, New Mexico is the author of *The Message of the Crystal Skull.* In her research, she had traveled to Mexico and enjoyed all the ruins but Teotihuacan, which she found depressing. In a past-life regression she experienced her life as a soldier in the ancient city:

"I was on the avenue about a third of the way from the Temple of the Moon, going toward the Temple of the Sun. It was jam-packed with fighting men using short swords. There was blood everywhere. I was overwhelmed with such a feeling of loss and pain that I began to sob uncontrollably and had to fight my way back to the present by telling myself over and over again, 'you are okay, you are alive, you made it.'

"I know I have to go back and relive that scene of the fight or it will dominate my memories. That is one of the reasons I am writing to you now, to get it out, on paper, to help clear my mind. I did manage to see the scene the day after, when the fight had ended and before the bodies were removed. (No wonder I found the place depressing!)"

Bette A. Cochran, Antlers, Oklahoma: "A gray-haired, muscular, thick-chested man came into the room. He was dressed in white, and there was some blue material on his chest, with gold trim on his sleeves. He came toward me carrying scrolls with crystal handles, and the leaves appeared to be thin metal of a gold or coppery hue."

Many others had also mentioned writing on thin sheets of metal, and I recalled a 1970s *Phoenix Republic* newspaper story about a scientific expedition in Mexico that found inscriptions on thin sheets of metal in a cave. It took me a while to look through my books on Atlantis and locate another mention of this. I finally found it in W. Scott-Elliot's *The Story of Atlantis:*

> The writing material of the Atlanteans consisted of thin sheets of metal, on the white porcelain-like surface of which the words were written. They also had the means of reproducing the written text by placing on the inscribed sheet another thin metal plate which had previously been dipped in some liquid. The text thus graven on the second plate could be reproduced at will on other sheets, a great number of which, when fastened together, constituted a book."

David Ritchey, Battleboro, Vermont: David visited Teotihuacan in 1981 while channeling for a parapsychology group.

"I am looking to the southeast to observe what is still visible of the pyramid in which the important material is stored. This is a set of records, not exactly in written form, but rather in three-dimensional block forms—rather like bricks—which, when properly assembled, create holographic images of the recorded data. The pyramid is approximately 2.7 miles away and is located close to the ridgeline of the southern edge of the valley."

Kathie Dame-Glerum, Camp Verde, Arizona: "There is a large central crystal to which each priest adds his knowledge by a placing on of hands. Each of the 'twelve' also has a smaller crystal—a ball—to program with specific knowledge. It takes only moments. But all the priests [books] could not be found. As a result, all the crystals were not programmed, and the large crystal was missing vital pieces of information."

Joyce Ketcherside, San Jose: "I'm high in the mountains, we're in a natural cave and going deep, very deep into the earth. We're hiding the 'Mother Crystal' and the 'Tablets.'"

Later, Joyce asks sadly, "Why can't the new ones accept our teachings? Why must they try to rule everyone?"

When I requested that people send me their Teotihuacan experiences I was afraid everyone might turn out to be a priest or priestess, but that was not the case. Most of my respondents described very ordinary lives.

Julie Pusateri, Solana Beach, California: "My occupation at that time was working with herbs—growing them, selling them, healing with them. I felt like I was in the healing arts and very good at it then."

Angie Rapalyea, Philadelphia: "I was a stone cutter. My wife and son and I lived in a small dwelling not far from the Avenue of the Dead. I worked on the facing stones that were part of the exterior facade of buildings. I was brown-skinned, wore sandals, a shirt, and a skirt—a simple man but with a real sense of my own dignity. I was proud to have my advice and designs sought after."

Barbara Olexer, North Hollywood: "I was a young matron, with long, straight, black hair, and I lived in a village south of Teotihuacan. My husband and I had several children. We were farmers, and our countryside was beautiful and the climate comfortable. We worshiped God, and our symbol for Him was the sun.

"The soldiers from Teotihuacan came and killed my husband and my children. They raped me many times. An officer took me for his concubine."

Vickie Lloyd, Hohenwald, Tennessee: "I lived on the Street of the Owls and wove cloth for robes. I had much to do because I also worked on the quilts that decorated the altars."

Many of the writers described their attire, or the attire of others observed in the frequent festivals.

Joseph B. Collins, West Sedona, Arizona: "I am a young male with a copper complexion, wearing a flapped garment (two flaps connected at the waist by a cord) with an intricately woven sunburst design. Around my neck is a sunburst symbol. My legs and arms are bare, and my body is what would be called today a 'swimmer's body.' On my feet I am wearing sandals with two straps at the back which wrap around my ankles. My hair is black, straight, and nearly shoulder length."

Kathy Lynn Douglass, Willow, Alaska: "Servant dressers were laying a cloak of iridescent feathers on a man's shoulders. The cloak was encrusted with gold and gems. His head was shaved on the sides, he wore sandals and a calf-length shift. Once in the cloak, he was handed a crystal wand. Then he stepped out of the shaded portico to address the gathering crowd."

Linda Lee Babry, Lake Ozark, Missouri: "To make a living I transferred pictures onto rugs of a cottonlike fabric which I handloomed. They were beautiful. I saw myself dressed in a white robe and sandals. My skin was dark like that of the Mayan people today. [Author's note: Maguey fiber was loomed for most of the clothes worn by Teotihuacanos.]

"Among my most vivid impressions was one of

eating a meal with my son. The meal consisted of white wafers, made from cornmeal. There was a blue substance as well, made from corn. We also ate cooked red beans. I observed myself bless the food with healing energy before we ate it."

Dietary reports from those sharing their past-life regressions were consistent with each other and with the archeological evidence. The basic diet consisted of corn, beans, and squash, seasoned with chili peppers and other spices. There is also evidence that tomatoes, avocados, pumpkins, and prickly-pear cactus were common foods. Occasionally this diet might be supplemented with fish from the river or nearby Lake Texcoco, wild dog, turkeys, jack rabbits, quail, deer, or birds. Dogs and turkeys were the only animals to be domesticated in Teotihuacan. Cacao beans, from which chocolate is derived, are native to the Gulf Coast and were a popular trade item with Teotihuacanos. The leaves are believed to have been chewed for a "lift."

As to the actual name of the once great city, many of those who wrote told me it started with an X, pronounced "Shh." But the way my correspondents attempted to spell it were many and varied. My own psychic investigations revealed the old name to be Xocoma, which is pronounced "Show-ko-ma."

The scope of peoples' reactions to these Teotihuacan regressions, and the kind of past-life information they received even when they had no conscious awareness of that once great civilization, is demonstrated in the following letter.

Sharee Thorne, Tasmania, Australia: "I'm thirty-four and have been receiving information through my Higher Self for about four years. Paul de Ruyter and I live on a forty-acre property outside of a country town in Tasmania, which is the only island state of

Australia—a beautiful island. We live near a river, and he works on a tugboat, taking large boats in and out of port. Paul received the *Master of Life* magazine in the post and took it off to work with him to read. He became really emotional while reading the article about Teotihuacan. I had not read the article before he directed me through the past-life regression.

"This was the most difficult regression I have ever experienced. I felt as if I actually became the entity in Mexico, and I had great difficulty overcoming the emotional pulls of the past. It left me feeling disturbed and 'not myself' for days afterward. Paul also said he felt very emotionally drained for days after reading the story. 'Like I need a good cry,' he said."

PORTIONS OF SHAREE'S REGRESSION, MAY 5, 1988

(Initially, Paul establishes that Sharee and he were part of what happened in Teotihuacan in A.D. 581, and goes on to ask her about her involvement. She explains that they were mates but their roles were reversed. Sharee was male and her name was pronounced "Kay-ur.")

Q. What was your vocation?

A. A builder. I build wash rooms . . . what you would call spas now.

Q. Can you describe the house we live in?

A. Two floors. No rooms.

Q. What was on the top level?

A. Sleeping quarters.

Q. Did we have any children?

A. No. We knew the end was near. It was not a time to bring children into the world.

Q. Were we associated with the spiritual hierarchy?

A. Only in that we accepted the teachings and knew the truth.

Q. What brought about the destruction of the truth?

A. The truth is never destroyed. But the priests were working with the dark forces. These were men who wanted power.

(Author's note: Sharee now goes on to describe the political changes that led to their deaths in the past life. Despite Paul's efforts to get her to focus on another event, she keeps returning to those traumatic times. He eventually commands her to return to an earlier time and to the house they shared, ". . . and you will not become emotionally involved," he directs.)

Q. All right, now I want you to think about this next question. Do you recall seeing any extraterrestrial flying ships?

A. Yes. They land frequently.

Q. Where do they come from?

A. Many places.

Q. From outer space? Other planets?

A. Yes.

Q. Why are they there?

A. To monitor.

CHAPTER ELEVEN

Preliminary Conclusions

Rather than documenting what happened at Teotihuacan from pieces of interrelated data, I've chosen to synthesize the information and present it as a story, beginning in the next section. Obviously, there is no way to prove anything that has not been established by archeologists, and even they often disagree on critical interpretations.

The conclusions that form the basis of the story are drawn from hundreds of past-life regressions and generally accepted historical evidence. Add to that the information contained in the Edgar Cayce readings, plus my personal psychic investigative techniques, including Higher Self sessions, automatic writing, and requested dreams. Tara also helped with much of this work, thanks especially to her great talent for automatic writing. It's a skill I often teach in seminars, but my wife has far surpassed me in her ability to contact various authorities on the other side.

The process of discovering metaphysically what happened 1400 years ago turned out to be a much different kind of search than I expected it to be. Armed with information from the past-life regressions and stacks of archeology and history books, I drew some rapid conclusions as to what, in general, had happened. But each regressed subject saw history (his story) through his own eyes and did not know what caused the major events. Huge pieces of the story were confused or completely lacking.

Tara and I soon found ourselves developing different historical/racial/spiritual/space people theories, running from the last days of Atlantis to Teotihuacan at its height—a period of at least 8600 years. Most were quite logical. But which, if any, were correct? Even before submitting the theories to our own psychic investigations, we tested them against Edgar Cayce's readings.

"The Sleeping Prophet's" clairvoyant discourses were given while in a self-induced hypnotic sleep state between 1901 and 1945. There were 14,263 readings in all, and of these, 9541 were related to health and medical conditions, while 1947 were life readings dealing with past and present lives. Major research studies have proven his health readings to be extremely accurate. Other Cayce readings also proved prophetic. A perfect example is one given on February 21, 1933, when he described the Atlantean Death Ray, a supersonic ray in which light was projected through a crystal. He said it would be rediscovered within twenty-five years, and in 1958 the laser gun was created in the United States.

If so many of Edgar Cayce's readings have been proven accurate, why not trust those we haven't yet proven? I decided to apply this line of reasoning as I reviewed the readings relating to Atlantis and Mesoamerica.

The Temple of Quetzalcoatl (Ket-sahl-koh-tl), the third most important structure in Teotihuacan, is magnificently wrought. It is decorated with carved stone heads of Quetzalcoatl, the "plumed serpent," alternating with heads of Tlaloc (Tlah-lok), the water god, thought by some archeologists to be a more important deity because he is "the giver of all life." Quetzalcoatl (known as Kukulcan to the Mayans and Huitzilopochtli to the Aztecs) was a great lawgiver and civilizer. There is no doubt that he once existed, because his image is found throughout the ancient Mesoamerican world. He was remembered as a compassionate king who preached love to his people.

Physical descriptions all portray Quetzalcoatl as exceptionally tall, and lighter-skinned than the Indians. He was said to have arrived from the east in a gleaming ship made of serpent skins—which might have been an Atlantean metal unknown to the aboriginal Indians of the Yucatan peninsula. Edgar Cayce scholars believe Quetzalcoatl was the Atlantean Iltar, who is said to have carried the Atlantean technology to the Yucatan, where he taught the religion of the Law of One and supervised the building of temples and pyramids. According to Mayan tradition, Quetzalcoatl returned many times to the eastern land to bring back books and art treasures.

In Reading 5750–1, Edgar Cayce said, "The first temples that were erected by Iltar and his followers [in Yucatan] were destroyed at the period of change physically in the contours of the land."

Archeological evidence supports the volcanic earth changes Cayce describes. And I remembered a 1970s afternoon spent with a Scottsdale, Arizona, shopowner who had the reputation of parachuting into remote Mexican archeological sites and sometimes smuggling out artifacts. He told me he had obtained the rights to uncover some above-ground archeological ruins, but instead he decided to dig down beneath them, where he found an even more ancient world.

"I broke through and into a huge room," he said.

"In it were many statues, six to seven feet tall. They were beautiful and in perfect condition."

"What did you do?" I asked.

"Much as I hated to, I covered them up and told no one in Mexico. They're too big to smuggle out, and important enough that the Mexicans would have killed me to get hold of them."

Immanuel Velikovsky once told *Science and Mechanics* magazine that prior civilizations are buried so deeply within the lower strata of the earth that we simply do not have archeological evidence of their existence.

"But we have abundant references in literature—even in rabbinical literature—that many times . . . before this present Earth Age existed, the *same* Earth was created—then it was leveled and recreated; all civilizations were buried," Velikovsky said.

Enough people survived the Mesoamerican earth changes to rebuild their lost world along the original architectural lines, but much of Atlantean culture and technology was forgotten in the centuries that followed. There was also a "mosaic effect" as people arrived in the Yucatan from the north, from Atlantis, from Lemuria, and from what is now South America. A new race evolved, and power-hungry priests created religious cults based upon fear and human sacrifice.

The Mayans of the Yucatan coexisted peacefully with their far more powerful neighbors, the inhabitants of Teotihuacan in central Mexico. Yet the Mayans were a bloodthirsty people who sought constant conquests, not because they needed the spoils of war or more land, but because they wanted prisoners to sacrifice to their gods. By contrast, extensive human sacrifice can only be verified in the early and later years of Teotihuacan.

If Edgar Cayce, Ruth Montgomery, Don Tinling, and a hundred past-life regression subjects were right about Mesoamerican contact with visitors from space, why would an advanced race of extraterrestrials who were voluntarily guiding and directing those cultures allow them to backslide into primitive cults that thrived on human sacrifice?

A bigger question is: Were extraterrestrials still in Mesoamerica at the time of Teotihuacan's rise to power? We know the city had a calendar more accurate than our own, and farmers used both astronomy and astrology to schedule plantings and harvests. People knew of the wheel; archeologists have found many wheeled toys, but there is no evidence that it was ever used for any practical purpose by adults. Also, wheels do not appear in any of the murals found throughout Mesoamerica.

So how did these people move giant stone blocks and timbers and build some of the most impressive monuments in history? I turn again to Edgar Cayce:

Reading 5750–1 says, "By lifting forces of those gases that are being used gradually in the present civilization, and by the fine work or activities of those versed in that pertaining to the source from which all power comes . . . For as long as there remain those pure in body, in mind, in activity, to the law of the One God, there is the continued resource for meeting the needs, or for commanding the elements and their activities in the supply of that necessary in such relations."

I didn't know what Cayce meant by that. Did the Teotihuacanos have an unknown way to lift or levitate provided by the extraterrestrials?

According to Cayce, Montgomery, and other metaphysical writers, extraterrestrials helped the Atlanteans create a way to harness the power of the sun using a giant crystal. The misuse of this death and/or propulsion ray was supposed to have triggered the earth changes that sank the island continent.

Maybe after that the extraterrestrials decided not to help immature societies develop potentially self-destructive technology. Perhaps when the aliens decided to continue interacting with earthlings, they chose only to monitor and provide guidance in safe areas, such as the construction of cities, the power of the mind, and techniques to record the progress of civilization (the calendar and how to store data in crystals).

Certainly there was highly evolved help in the design and construction of Teotihuacan, for it did not slowly grow to be a great city/state but was the product of a master plan. In her book, *The Great Migration,* author Vada F. Carlson says:

> In the great valley of Mexico, near a large navigable lake called Texcoco, they began construction of their city of Teotihuacan, now being brought, little by little, into full perspective. How greatly they planned—the immense span of their perception—is shown by the area they chose and the groundwork they did. The whole two-mile by three-and-a-half-mile city site was smoothed, then paved with consecutive floors of cementlike plaster. Within this huge rectangle they built the Pyramid of the Moon, the much larger Pyramid of the Sun, the Temple of Quetzalcoatl, and the citadel.

"Would you check out our latest set of conclusions with your sources?" I asked Tara, handing her a rough draft of this chapter. It was a rare Saturday afternoon in July, when the house wasn't overrun with kids and friends. The baby was taking her nap.

"Sure, I'll do it right now," she said.

"I think a lot of the energy for this book is coming from my own spirit guide and the tribe," I said.

Tara often communicates with my guide, plus her own guides and others in an altered-state environment she calls her "temple room."

After receiving automatic writing for over an hour in the studio, Tara returned to the living room. She was all smiles, describing the joyful gathering of our guides and Cheyenne's guide, who was Tara's recently deceased great grandmother. After some advice on other matters, my guide took control of Tara's pen. The following is a part of the communication.

"Yes, the book is going in the direction that we want it to go, but there are a few facts missing. You and Richard incarnated in different sequences in Teotihuacan, and together in the 500s as priests. This was your last incarnation in the city, and you were happy not to return in following lifetimes. You did, however, live in the Inca and Aztec civilizations. It can all blend together on the earth plane.

"As for human sacrifice, it was something that the peaceful priests of your time tried to abolish, but it was reestablished after 581.

"Quetzalcoatl was a powerful warrior who originally came to conquer the barbarians, but saw that he could mesmerize them with his looks and modern Atlantean technology. He became a legend to the simplest of minds. He wore feather plumes around his neck, which made him the plumed serpent, a symbol of heaven and earth. His trips back and forth to Atlantis were to gather the additional technology that kept him from being killed. For him the trips were for his own survival and for that of his men. But the Indians made him a god.

"The wheel was not used in Mesoamerica. But they did use a type of pulley system that set huge stones on large ropes, and then many men pulled back and forth to get the stones where they wanted them. They did not levitate anything. It was all a very basic way of handling things." [Note: Further research disclosed pulley systems were used in Mesoamerica.]

"As for the aliens, indeed they were part of what happened in Atlantis and Teotihuacan, and your theories are quite accurate. Extraterrestrials are among you now. But they are not interested in helping you technically. They realize that as a people you are not ready for them and may never be. Richard's work does not relate to aliens. He is here to guide people out of their own ruts, just as you have helped him out of many of his." [Note: My guide ended the communication with information about our business and personal lives.]

With the aforementioned conclusions and this new information in mind, I begin my story of Xocoma (Teotihuacan) in late summer of the year A.D. 580. . . .

SECTION

III

The Story of
Teotihuacan/Xocoma

CHAPTER TWELVE

A.D. 580

The throbbing drumbeats echoed through Narlo's dreams, wresting him out of sleep and into the dark reality of his windowless room. He sat up, rubbed his eyes, acknowledged the stiffness in his back, and inhaled a hint of smoke. A faint light came from the hallway, and Narlo slipped into a tunic and made his way through two rooms to the patio. Cugal and several others of the apartment were already looking up toward the great Mu Pyramid.

"Xcane is dying," Cugal said, as Narlo placed his hand on his friend's shoulder.

The first rays of dawn streaked across the valley and reflected off the top of the shimmering white pyramid, sending random stabs of light into the awakening city below. A huge, round billow of smoke rose into the air from the top of the structure. It was soon followed by another, then another, sending the news into the sky for distant eyes to read. Unseen were the relentless drummers, pounding out the thunderous "death beat" that fell like a fist on Narlo's chest and seemed to hammer the life force from his body.

As they stood on the patio, the observers could see

the north side of the pyramid. On top were the twin temples, one dedicated to the god Talote, "Giver of All Life," and one dedicated to Xcane, wise ruler of Xocoma. In front of the temples rose the towering statue of Talote, carved from a single block of purplish-red, crystal-encrusted porphyry. In front of the statue was the fire pit.

"The council will be meeting," Narlo said.

"A runner has already been here," Cugal replied. "We have two hours to prepare."

Thirteen priests plus eighteen servants and retainers lived in the apartment compound. Each priest had a small room at ground level, while those who served them lived in four large rooms in the basement. The compound was built of stone, with solid walls that faced the street. Beautifully carved pillars supported the overhanging roof of the apartments, and the walls, plastered with white gesso, were polished to a high sheen and painted with beautiful murals. The sleeping rooms formed a maze leading to the communal bath and to an outside patio located in the center of the complex. In the middle of the patio was an altar, on the east side a roofed prayer temple, and on the west side the eating area. The patio floor was a mortar of pounded red volcanic stone, and it sloped slightly to a hole that emptied into the cistern.

Of the thousands of priests in Xocoma, the thirteen who lived here were numbered among the fifty-two men who constituted the First Priest Caste. They were the religious leaders of the Xocoma nation, center of the civilized world. The fifty-two answered only to Xcane himself and to the combined voice of his seven sons.

The bath, usually a place of good-natured conversation, was quiet today. Narlo and Cugal hung their tunics on hooks along the wall and joined two other priests, already sitting in the waist-deep water. Narlo shivered, and wondered if it was because of the cold water or the fear he felt regarding what was to come. Through the pillars he could see some of the other priests still standing in the patio and staring up at the pyramid. Their pained expressions betrayed their thoughts.

The chilly water shocked Narlo's muscles back to life. Now that he was in his middle thirties, sleeping on a maguey fiber pallet was a spiritual discipline he had begun to question when he awoke in the morning feeling stiffer than usual. The two priests who had been sharing the bath with them left, and were replaced by two others. As was their custom, Narlo and Cugal washed each other's hair. Narlo leaned his head back until the water covered his ears. Every morning for eight years he had studied the ceiling mural of the bathhouse as his friend gently massaged his temples and the nape of his neck. But today there was no teasing, no joy. Even the mural, always so friendly, seemed to take on a different meaning. Bordering the square ceiling were stylized turquoise waves, and in the center rose an island upon which naked men fished the waters and lounged under bountiful fruit trees. Servants were preparing a feast. Colorful birds perched in the trees. Butterflies filled the sky. Narlo loved the mural, but today it seemed to warn of a way of life about to sink beneath the waves of change.

As he dried himself, still troubled by his sense of foreboding, Narlo could not help admiring his friend's muscular nakedness, which embodied the Xocoma ideal of masculine beauty. Cugal was three years younger than Narlo, but both men were of the Cumquic race that ruled Xocoma, and both had shoulder-length black hair and intense black eyes.

Narlo and Cugal shared a relationship of total acceptance and unquestioned mutual support that dated back to their early days as novice priests in training. They were both the sons of successful merchants who aspired to have their children attain the most respected level of Xocoman society—the First Caste priesthood.

"Formal dress, master?" asked Tanzel, Narlo's fourteen-year-old servant boy, who stood in the doorway of the bathhouse. Cugal's servant boy was behind him.

Narlo nodded and turned to allow the boy to dress him in a loincloth and short white kilt. Next, Tanzel placed the sacred symbol, fashioned from inlaid jade and obsidian, around his master's neck. A short white tunic with matching gold ribbing and sandals completed Narlo's attire for the council meeting.

The piercing wail of conch trumpets now joined the echoing drums, and the mournful notes of a flute seemed to issue from just beyond the walls of the compound. The smell of frying corn cakes wafted through the patio. Several of the priests had foregone their morning meal to pray in the temple, but Narlo and Cugal sat down at the eating table. Their servant boys quickly brought each of them a platter of corn cakes topped with slices of avocado, and a cup of water. While their masters ate, the boys began the daily task of arranging the older men's hair, weaving it into three rows of braids across the front and drawing the rest back into a long fall adorned with a seashell clip.

"I'd like to see Nlers before the meeting," Narlo said.

"Agreed," Cugal replied.

Narlo and Cugal left the compound through the alley door that led to the Street of Balam-Ti, which they crossed before continuing down the alley to the Lord's Way, the great street that ran from the base of the Oag Pyramid, past the immense Mu Pyramid, through blocks of beautiful temples, palaces, and eventually across the river to Palace Square, which enclosed the Temple of the Plumed Serpent and the dual palaces of government.

The Lord's Way was a street used only by priests, except on special ritual occasions or during festivals. Today, Narlo noticed, it was filled with priests of all castes, their rank indicated by their attire and hairstyle. One of a lower caste could not address one of a higher caste unless first spoken to by his superior. As he passed through the crowd, Narlo could see in their faces the questions they wanted to ask but could not. Some were crying. Others were praying. And above the confusion the drums drove the reality deeper and deeper into the consciousness of the citizens of Xocoma.

The dying Xcane, Lord of Xocoma, was eighty-four years old. He had ruled since he was twenty-seven. "It would be a rare priest who has previously experienced the transference of power," Narlo said.

"I had no idea there were so many priests in the city," Cugal replied, elbowing his way through a group that was blocking the entire street.

"Obviously, they've come in from every compound temple," said Narlo, noting the fear in their eyes. "The marketplace will be madness."

Nlers lived with his daughter in the Palace of the Wise Ones—a beautiful compound on the Lord's Way, between the Mu Pyramid and Palace Square. It was home to a dozen of the people who once came from the sky in flying ships and today helped to guide the Xocomans with higher knowledge. To live in the earth environment the Wise Ones had to step into the bodies of humans who offered themselves for this purpose. Nlers had stepped into the vehicle of a tall man from a faraway mountain civilization—a descendant of the ancient Lemurians, who were hermaphrodites.

Because of the difficulty in finding volunteers willing to allow the aliens to "step in," the dozen Wise Ones represented nearly as many different races. Yet underneath they were all peace-loving Pheladians—a race that had interacted with earth people since the beginning of time. Many of the Wise Ones had taken earth mates, further diversifying the racial mix within the palace compound. Narlo felt that the occupants of this palace reflected the racial mix of Xocoma, which gave his nation a unique strength and power.

Narlo and Cugal walked up the stairs, past four uniformed soldiers, and entered the palace through giant pillars carved to represent a deity unknown to the people of Xocoma. The white walls of the temple were polished to such a sheen that Narlo could see his own reflection as they traversed the hallway leading into the apartment compound and temples. This was one of the few places in the city with an open expanse of unadorned space that was not painted with murals.

The hallway opened into a flowered courtyard filled with milling people. Narlo saw Xtah, Nlers's seven-year-old daughter, playing nearby with some other children. "Hello, Xtah. Where's your daddy?" he asked.

The seven-year-old's face lit up like a sun flare as she ran to Narlo, jumping into his arms, and reaching out to hug Cugal as well.

"Mmmmmm," she purred. "Daddy's in his room, but he's not happy today."

"Mmmmmm," the men responded. "Tell him we're here, Xtah, please."

She smiled and ran off through the crowd, but was soon back again and asked Narlo and Cugal to follow her.

Nlers rose from his writing table to greet his good friends, embracing them with bold hugs. "What we have feared for so long is coming to pass," he said, gesturing to two chairs. Xtah stood in the doorway. "Xtah, fetch our guests a bowl of cool water." The child smiled and was gone.

Narlo had seen no other Lemurian like Nlers. He was nearly seven heads tall, with broad shoulders, wideset green eyes, and long raven hair that extended to the middle of his back. He walked with a big man's swagger that was not in keeping with his gentle personality.

On one side of Nlers's table sat a clear quartz crystal, over a foot tall. It glowed blue in the sunlight that reflected off the shiny walls, down the hallway, and into the room. A star map decorated the wall above the table. On the far side of the room there was a raised bed and a mattress filled with bird feathers. Narlo looked at it longingly.

"We've been blessed with fifty-seven years of rule by a kindly Lord who has always managed to exercise control over his heirs, though often with great difficulty," Nlers said.

"A figurehead lord," Narlo corrected. "Wise in that he allowed Xocoma to be ruled by a democratic council of men who love equality and peace."

"Xcane carried on the traditions of his grandfather," Cugal said. "We can't deny him that."

"I don't deny Xcane's wisdom," Narlo said. "But it's the Xocoman Council that has balanced the needs of the people with the needs of a ruling nation. For two hundred years no other nation has dared to challenge Xocoma. Yet they battle endlessly with each other and annually sacrifice more souls than live in this city."

"And in our time much of the credit for peace goes to you, Narlo." Nlers sat back in his carved wooden chair and smiled lovingly.

"Not any more than to the two of you and the other thirteen of the Atlantean Council."

"But as the elected leader, Narlo, you bear the brunt of the resistance," Cugal said.

"Which marks you now," Nlers added. "When the drums stop, the jaguar will begin to roar."

"Can the Pheladians help us to maintain what is?" Narlo asked.

"We can only provide you with the kind of assistance you are already receiving. Our noninterference pact was made thousands of years ago. Personally, my knowledge is only of crystal record keeping."

Xtah returned with a bowl of water, which the three men shared by passing it in a circle until it was gone.

"I have something for you, Narlo," Nlers said. "Xtah, on the shelf in the next room is a rod. Please bring it to me."

Xtah returned, proudly holding a thick jade rod with a crystal end. She handed it to her father, who raised it high in the air, his arm stiff, held it there momentarily, and then slowly lowered it before giving it to Narlo.

"It's beautiful, Nlers. I don't know what to say." The jade rod was the length of Narlo's forearm and carved to represent a coiled serpent. At the feathered head, growing out of the serpent's mouth, was a finger-length quartz crystal.

"It's more than beautiful, it's perfectly balanced," Nlers replied. "Use it wisely."

Narlo stood and slowly raised the rod, holding it horizontally in front of him. He closed his eyes, took a deep breath, and began to concentrate his bodily life force in the area below his navel, then he drew it up and into his right arm, down into his hand and out into the crystal, which began to glow. Within moments it was a bright, shimmering blue that seemed to pulsate, sending energy crackling into the room.

Cugal could feel his scalp begin to tingle. Xtah moved closer to her father.

With a snap of his wrist, Narlo tilted the rod straight up and the glow diminished. "They'll want the knowledge."

"They must not get it," Nlers said.

CHAPTER THIRTEEN

Uniformed soldiers lined the west side of the Lord's Way from the river to the end of Market Square, directly facing the hordes of people that peered toward Palace Square in frightened expectation. Commerce was at a standstill. High atop the walls of the fortresslike enclosure, Narlo and Cugal stopped momentarily to observe the situation across the street.

On a normal day Market Square and the surrounding area was a center of barter and trade. Merchants laid out their goods on benches or ground cloths, while the stalls of food sellers covered many blocks and offered fruit, vegetables, and condiments. In season there was an abundance of pumpkins, tomatoes, beans, avocados, and prickly-pear cactus, and herbs raised in patio gardens were also sold here. Corn, of course, was supplied by the state to all the citizens of Xocoma. Occasionally, although the price was high, you could purchase fish, meat, and live animals—usually wild dogs or turkeys. On most days you could also find a few sellers from the southern jungles offering exotic birds, snakes, and monkeys. Beyond them sat the pottery merchants and the cloth-weaving women who spun or loomed their wares for the wealthy. Leather products were scarce and expensive, but rabbitskin coats were the rarest of all the many items offered for sale, and also the most desired, for winter was cold and the apartment compounds were not heated. In smaller sections of the Market Square craftsmen displayed finely modeled obsidian razors, knives, darts, and arrowheads. And one could always find jewelry made of gold and gemstones, cosmetics, brightly colored feathers and feather products, medicines, rope, cord, and thread.

But this was no normal market day. Narlo doubted that the populace that had flooded into the selling zone understood the reason for the thundering drums and the billowing balls of smoke that ascended to the heavens. Rumors were probably spreading like a fire through fall leaves, and he understood the importance of a public declaration.

Beyond Market Square and the distant apartment compounds the world looked the same. The towering, snowcapped mountain snagged passing clouds as always in the month of Calk, as summer drew to a close. Above, an eagle swooped out of the azure sky, catching a defenseless bird on the wing.

A bad sign, Narlo thought as he turned and descended the steps into Palace Square. The two men marched directly across the immense compound to the Temple of the Plumed Serpent. Artistically, the structure was the grandest in all of the Xocoma empire. Six ornately carved tiers ascended to the elaborately decorated temple, where two-dozen cult priests prayed in never-ending rotation. Alternate tiers displayed massive carvings of the Plumed Serpent and the god Talote. To the left of the structure was the Palace of Government, to the right, the Palace of Prayer.

Kneeling on the sacred circles at the foot of the temple, Narlo and Cugal offered their private prayers to the gods and touched a finger to earth, then to the center of their foreheads. When they had finished, they stood, bowed three times, and walked to the Palace of Prayer. It was nearly time for the council meeting, and most of the fifty-two had already taken their assigned seats.

Even here, the drumming deadens the senses, Narlo thought as he sat in the front row, waiting. The white room was built to accommodate the First Caste priests of the Xocoman Council. At the end of the room, facing the audience, was an intricately carved stone speaker's platform supported on one side by Talote and on the other by the Plumed Serpent. A colorful mural covered the wall behind the platform: Talote was shown dressed in a huge feather headdress, his upper face resembling a bird, while white fangs protruded from his mouth. From his hands flowed drops of water, the source of life. To each side of the god marched a procession of figures dressed in animal costumes—spotted dogs, coyotes, jaguars, and giant birds.

Narlo sat in silence, listening to the nervous hum that surrounded him like a gathering cloud. The priests, dressed identically and wearing their hair in three frontal braids, were talking in hushed tones. Few were praying.

From the back of the room an ocarina musician started to play a mantra, and the others soon fell silent. At the comforting sound of the familiar notes, the sacred words began to resonate through Narlo's mind. A young man carrying a bowl of smoldering herbs walked slowly up the center aisle, and, as the fragrance assailed their nostrils, the priests closed their eyes to hum.

"Ohmmmm nama talaaaaa, ohmmmm nama shelaaaa." The mantra began as a quiet, soothing sound that grew and intensified until it swept through the room, filling the chanting men with waves of vibrational energy. The energy currents entered the top of Narlo's head and settled momentarily in the center of his forehead. Then, in a rush, they poured down into his throat, his heart, his solar plexus, his spleen, and the base of his spine. Narlo was remotely aware that all sounds faded away and his senses were numbed just before the explosive surge of serpent fire ascended his spine to flood his body and mind with power and awareness.

When the chanting ended, the singer of holy songs began. Narlo inhaled slowly to a count of eight, held the breath to a count of four, exhaled to a count of eight, and again counted to four before inhaling. His body became so charged with psychic energy that he had to consciously block the flow of any of his life force into the new wand, which he held securely in his lap.

Cabran the Elder, Master Speaker of the Xocoman Council, was standing in the center of the speaker's platform when the priests opened their eyes. He was in his seventies and wore the three-braided hairstyle of the council priests, but the rest of his white hair flowed down his back, nearly to his waist. Even though his body was bowed and he had difficulty standing for long periods, his lined face radiated love as he led the opening prayer and performed the protective ritual. "And now to our sad task," he said. "Our Lord Xcane is not expected to live until sunset. His doctor is with him. His seven sons are with him. Talote awaits him on the other side." He bowed his head momentarily before continuing. "Each of you is to meet immediately with your precinct priests to inform them of the situation and what is to come. They in turn are to inform the people of their compounds."

Each of the fifty-two was responsible for fifty compound priests. There were over two thousand apartment compounds in the city, and they all housed between seventy-five and three hundred people and included a temple within the walled grounds, with one or more priests assigned to each compound. When the conch trumpets relayed their message throughout the city, all the priests reported to their assigned locations.

"The trumpets will issue the call one hour after this council meeting is adjourned. The message is as follows: First, Xcane is dying of the breathing difficulty that has plagued him for so long. He is not expected to awaken from the transcending sleep. Second, in the absence of the Lord of Xocoma, Xcane's sons will assume the position of Lord as a Council of Seven. They will have sixty days to choose a successor among their number. Third, the public prayer hours are to be doubled and all priests are to prepare for the rituals of mourning."

As Cabran the Elder sat down to open the forum for discussion, the wooden doors at the back of the palace burst open and Khatic, eldest son of Xcane, strode into the room wearing a jaguar-head mantle and feathered headdress. A jade breastplate hung around his neck, and the rattles of snakes formed a belt around his leather loincloth. In his hand was a spear; to his left and right stood three uniformed soldiers. The room tensed and grew silent.

"Yes?" asked Cabran the Elder.

"I'm only here to observe," replied Khatic in a loud voice. "Please continue."

Cabran the Elder rose in silent disbelief.

Khatic raised the spear in a slow, sinister motion, then let the blunt end fall to the floor. It landed with a sharp thud that echoed through the room. "Continue," he roared.

Narlo stood and stepped into the aisle, facing

Khatic at a distance of twenty yards. The priest's body trembled with outrage at the intrusion. "You break the law of the Xocoman Council even before your father has crossed over?"

"At a time like this there is no need to stand on ceremony, Atlantean."

"At a time like this there is more reason than ever to uphold the law. This council will never meet in the presence of anyone who is not a member."

"It is a time for changes." Khatic's deep voice boomed off the walls. He raised his spear and brought it crashing down three more times. The soldiers fanned out, holding their spears ready. "Continue!"

"Leave!" Narlo said quietly. Cugal was now at his side, and other priests quickly joined him—first four, then seven, then a dozen or more.

Narlo and Khatic stood silently, glaring at each other. Khatic's black eyes shone with the madness of too much pulque, too many coca leaves, and too many morning-glory seeds, which leave behind a head full of bad dreams. The intruder's lids narrowed at the outer corners and his lips twisted into a sadistic smile. He flicked his tongue across his teeth, savoring an opportunity to release years of pent-up rage.

Narlo breathed deeply, emptied his mind and projected a scan line to discern his adversary's intent. The words echoed in his head. *Killing the Atlantean will intimidate the pious fools.*

As Khatic stepped toward him, Narlo raised the jade and crystal rod and was surprised how quickly the crystal began to glow. "Leave!" he commanded once again.

Khatic laughed—a deep, demented laugh that chilled the bones of the fifty-two—and rushed forward. He was lifting his spear when the full force of Narlo's will, projected and amplified by the crystal, struck the intruder's body, throwing him backward to the ground. The spear clattered onto the floor, and the jaguar headdress rolled away like a cowering animal trying to escape. The soldiers, who had not moved, looked at each other, at Khatic lying in shock on the ground, at the glowing crystal rod, and at the fire in Narlo's eyes. Then all but one bolted out the doors of the Palace of Prayer.

Narlo and the others turned their backs on the prone Khatic and returned to their seats. The ocarina musician began to play another mantra. The priests closed their eyes, chanting "Ohmmm nama Taalootee" over and over in ascending harmonies that drifted out through the open doors and across the courtyard of Palace Square. As the sound reached the ears of the people in Market Square, a hush descended on the throng. When the priests opened their eyes, Khatic was gone . . . but his spear remained, still quivering as if in silent fury, where it had pierced the sacred symbol embedded in the floor at the outer entrance to the palace.

CHAPTER FOURTEEN

"The assembly of the Atlantean Circle is formally in session," said Narlo to the fifteen hooded, robed figures who sat cross-legged in a ring around him. The splintered wood torches tossed eerie shadows on the rough walls of the cave. Resting on the hard-packed earth in the center of the circle, a panel of crystals emitted a high-pitched hum as it glowed and pulsed iridescent blue.

The fourteen men and two women held hands and chanted a mantra. Ten of the group were of the fifty-two. Nlers and Xpico represented the Wise Ones, while the artisans, the growers, the builders, and the merchants had each sent one of their number to speak for them.

Narlo mentally blocked out any extraneous sensations: the scent of burning torches, the "slap-slap" of dripping water, the penetrating dampness of the cave. The past was alive and breathing in the surrounding darkness. He could feel it filling the present with heightened awareness. As his mind stilled, the light from the torches revealed the changing faces around the circle. Visions of the ancestors merged with the features of his friends and then dissolved again into the shadowy light. Cugal's face became a stern old man, a beautiful woman in her prime, and the loving face of his guide-in-spirit.

"Xcane is here," whispered Nlers. His eyes grew big as he stared into oblivion. The others twice raised and lowered their heads.

Mentally opening to channel, Nlers's vocal cords strained to convert discarnate projections into earthly words, which at first sounded like the hoarse call of a crow. "Your . . . your . . . your power is your knowledge. Use it peacefully to combat the darkness I see descending. The will of the people of Xocoma will be your strength or your destruction." For several moments there was only the hum of the crystals and dripping of dark water. "They tell me I must go."

Narlo's own breathing sounded like a driving windstorm in the strange silence that always followed discarnate contact. A sadness welled up within him at the thought of Xcane's death. It penetrated his body like an obsidian knife, opening the wound of his painful memories of many meetings with the Lord of the Xocoma nation.

The day Narlo was elected to the Xocoman Council of fifty-two, Xcane had called him to the Royal Palace to partake of food and drink. They had talked of many things, but primarily of the importance of maintaining peace. "You can conquer with weapons or you can conquer with commerce," Xcane had said. "Commerce is the more powerful of the two. Add to that a fair and just religion that gives people hope, and you provide an order that can only be destroyed from within."

Narlo had been chosen from all the Second Caste priest candidates because of his highly developed mental powers and his impassioned support for Xcane's philosophy. Two years later he was again summoned to the Royal Palace by his Lord. "You know of the Atlantean Circle?" Xcane asked him.

"I know only that it's a powerful secret organization whose Master Speaker is Kal-Peu," Narlo replied. "No one knows the identity of the other members."

"There are hundreds of secret societies in Xocoma, Narlo. Some I know of, but many I don't. Unless they are subversive, I am unconcerned. But the Atlantean Circle is a very special organization of my grandfather's creation. How do you respond to mention of the name?"

"With respect, my Lord. In meetings of the Xocoman Council, when Kal-Peu speaks as the circle's representative, he wields more influence than anyone but the Elder."

"And rightfully so, for the Atlantean Circle is comprised of the most powerful members of the Xocoman Council, as well as Pheladians and representatives of the different occupations our citizens pursue. All but the elected leader remain anonymous for reasons of security. Only I know their identities. They always meet in secret."

"Why are you telling me this, my Lord?"

"Kal-Peu died suddenly in the night."

"Oh, no!"

"Mourning will come later, Narlo. At this moment I am concerned with the opening in the Atlantean Circle of sixteen. It must be closed immediately, and I nominated you for that position. The circle has voted, and you were unanimously approved. There was not one dissenting vote."

Narlo sat in silence, not knowing how to respond.

"Do you accept membership in the Atlantean Circle?" Xcane asked, placing his hand on Narlo's.

"Yes, my Lord, if it serves you."

Xcane sat back and smiled, a sincere smile. "Well-spoken. It does serve me." His hand swept across an obsidian chime, beckoning a servant who hurried into the room.

"The sacred drink," Xcane said.

Moments later the servant returned with two elaborate potter's mugs of freezing cold snow covered with pulque, a fermented juice of the maguey plant. Xcane raised his mug and Narlo did the same.

"A toast to your continued service to the people of our nation," Xcane said.

Narlo smiled, lowered his eyes and sipped the drink. "How is this possible, my Lord?" he said, nodding at the mound of crystalline ice that filled his mug.

Xcane laughed. "Each morning runners in relay bring it from the mountaintop in thick clay casks packed in dry grass. It is delicious, is it not?"

Narlo nodded.

"There will be a meeting tonight of the Atlantean Circle to elect a new Master Speaker. All sixteen members must be present for this vote. Nlers, the Wise One, will come to your compound an hour after sundown. Be ready to go with him."

It was three years later that death claimed another member of the circle. At that time, Narlo convinced Xcane to nominate Cugal and he was accepted. Soon after, Narlo was elected "The Atlantean," or Master Speaker to the Xocoman Council and the people of Xocoma.

Nlers coughed sharply, pulling Narlo back to the present. He breathed deeply and noticed the smoke of the torches had floated to the roof of the cave and was hanging like a ghostly canopy over the circle.

"The circle is open," Narlo said softly.

"First, I am concerned for your safety," Cugal told him. "Khatic tried to kill you in the presence of the council, and you made a fool of him. By now his soldiers will surely have spread the story throughout the city. He will come for you again."

"I don't think so," said Xpico, the Wise One. She had assumed the body of a woman of white skin, a race rarely seen in Xocoma. "Khatic may be the eldest son, but any of the other six are wiser than he. He was probably drunk on his own wrathful dreams and acted from his own frustration."

Narlo nodded in agreement.

Xpico continued. "I anticipate that the others, who have surely heard what happened, will be able to control Khatic. The seven will not risk turning the entire population of our nation against them. And I don't think they will want to pit their physical force against our superior mental powers. Instead, they will begin a campaign of rumors to get what they want."

"What do they want?" asked Alita, the other female member of the circle, and the representative of the artisans. Beginning at her hairline was a painted red stripe the width of two fingers. It ran down the left side of her face, across her eye, and down her cheek. Narlo had never seen her without it.

"They want the full power of leadership," Cugal said. "Once they have elected the new Lord from their number, they will not be content to maintain what is. Until today the Xocoman council has made all the important decisions about matters of state. The furtherance of commerce and of missionary work in the service of our God are always the first priorities. But the new Lord will want to do things his own way, and that will probably be the way of the Jaguar."

"Five of the seven are members of the Jaguar Clan," noted another member of the circle.

"Much to the consternation of their father," Narlo said. "I don't know if Xcane ever accepted the existence of a divine, loving God, but he knew the importance of such a symbol to the success of our nation. While our religion teaches that the many deities of our people are different aspects of Talote, the Jaguar Clan sees them as different gods . . . angry, vengeful gods that reward in direct proportion to the number of bloody sacrifices offered upon the altar."

Narlo knew that the sixteen were already aware of this, but he felt the need to speak the words. He visualized the bloody Mayans and Zapotecs as he spoke, and shuddered at the thought of their countless human sacrifices. During his lifetime the only such sacrifices in Xocoma had been convicted criminals deserving of their fate. Each spring, after dying upon the altar, one of them was skinned, and the Black Priest wore the skin to perform a sacred dance at the Planting Festival. Narlo was disgusted by this last remaining vestige of the old ways and had twice tried to convince the council to ban the practice, but both times he had failed.

"What of the propaganda the seven will surely concoct?" asked a member.

Nlers answered. "They will use any misfortune to their advantage. They will claim that had the gods been appeased with sacrificial blood, the difficulty would not have arisen . . . the gods would have been benevolent."

"You envision, then, a long-lasting conflict between the House of the Lord and the Xocoman Council?" asked one of the members.

"Yes," said Narlo.

"Yes," said Cugal.

"Yes," said Nlers and Xpico and several others.

"What of the powers?" Cugal asked.

"This is no longer a time of connection," Nlers said. He was referring to Atlantean times, when the people were linked psychically. But when the connection was misused by power-hungry leaders, the people were forced to disconnect. "Today, the powers are available to all First and Second Caste priests who are willing to devote the time and energy necessary to develop them. Of course, some will have more natural ability than others, but the power is available to all."

"Personally, I don't think any of the seven has the self-discipline to develop the powers, even if he were tutored," Narlo said. "But there is little doubt that they will attempt to draw to their side priests already proficient in the use of these powers. I am afraid that we can almost certainly anticipate negative mind projection."

"Priests of first magnitude power will never collaborate," Cugal insisted.

The sixteen nodded their heads in agreement.

"As keeper of the crystal records I fear for their safety and for the safety of the knowledge that they contain," said Nlers.

"The knowledge can only be accessed by the sixteen of us," someone pointed out.

"If necessary, they can be hidden," suggested someone else.

"I suppose so," Nlers replied sadly. He stepped into the center of the circle, seated himself in front of the pulsating panel and placed his hands on the crystal rods, forcing one down several inches. The pulsing intensified, the light dimmed almost to darkness and then burst forth with dazzling intensity. While the fifteen in the outer circle held hands, the Wise One programmed the content of the meeting into the panel.

When Nlers had finished the programming, Narlo asked, "Can you draw upon the crystals for knowledge of any similar circumstances that may have existed in Atlantean times?"

"I will try," Nlers said. Once again placing his hands on the panel, he closed his eyes and breathed deeply. Time passed and the crystals hummed and pulsed from light to dark in the near silence of the cave. Nlers had taught all the members how to use their mental powers to draw memories out of the programmed crystals, but he was still the most talented time channel of the sixteen. When he began to speak, his voice was raspy and without emotion. "In the Poseidan time of conflict between the Sons of the Law of One and the Sons of Belial . . . I see . . . I feel . . . and I sorrow. Those of Belial withdraw from the Order of One into a Temple of Darkness from which tentacles of fear spread across the land." Nlers, his head tilted to the side until it almost touched his shoulder, his face distorted in a grimace, swallowed hard and breathed in short, shallow gasps.

"In an attempt to control their world, they misused the powers, channeling the sun's rays into the great crystals in the pit, which resonated with influences deep inside the earth. Thus were the destructive forces unleashed and the terrible earth changes of the breaking up of the land. This I see as in a mirror, and I tremble."

Nlers was silent. Finally Narlo spoke. "Those are powers we know nothing of."

"They were the same forces of light and darkness that oppose each other today. And many ways exist to shatter and disperse the continents," Nlers said.

"Can you tell us again of the One whose name is pronounced Ohm?" Narlo said.

Nlers, his eyes still closed, raised his head a little. His face relaxed and took on a look of serene contemplation. "The One God whose name is pronounced Ohm teaches his followers that they shall live again and again upon the earth. With the exception of Xpico and me, those of the circle have lived many times in the Atlantean lands, as you have lived many times in the lands of your present world. Each life is for learning and with each life comes new opportunities.

"The One God whose name is pronounced Ohm teaches his followers that they are responsible for all that they experience upon the earth. The cumulative effect of their thoughts and deeds over many lifetimes has created their present circumstances.

"The One God whose name is pronounced Ohm teaches his followers that they are all part of him and of the whole, so that to judge another is to judge yourself. To fear another is to fear yourself. To love another is to love yourself.

"The One God whose name is pronounced Ohm, who was with you in Atlantis and in Mayan lands, is with you again now in Xocoma as you meet your past and face the tests you have ordained."

Nlers sat upright with a start and his eyes opened wide. The fifteen others were looking at him expectantly, but no more words were spoken. He returned to his position in the circle and they all joined hands, synchronizing their breathing until their lungs rose and fell as one. Xpico started to hum the mantra, which floated up into the darkness and rolled through the empty caverns of the cave until it reached the farthest limits of space, then reverberated back to the chanters like the song of the heavenly spheres.

The sixteen left the cave through the two separate entrances, one beneath Nlers's study on the Street of Zaquicaz, and the other at the basement level of the small apartment compound shared by six priests of the circle. Before the closing ritual, Narlo had warned them, "Be careful! You can no longer assume that you are not being followed or overheard."

When the others were gone, Narlo, Cugal, Xpico, and Nlers sat in Nlers's study in the glow of a small lamp. "I will prepare a plan to hide the records if it becomes necessary," Nlers said.

The other three nodded their heads in agreement.

"Will your people return for you if such a time should come?" Cugal asked.

"You are my people now," Nlers replied, placing his large hand on Cugal's knee. "After all these years and the birth of my daughter, after my many acts of intent, I've tied my destiny to this earth."

As Narlo and Cugal stepped out Nlers's front door into the moonlight, Narlo thought he caught a glimpse of a figure lurking in the shadows by the far wall.

CHAPTER FIFTEEN

"They've journeyed overland for twenty days after eleven days at sea and five days making their way through the jungle from Kaminta to meet their ship," said Cabran the Elder, as Narlo and Cugal listened intently. The three friends were eating lunch at a crowded outdoor restaurant in Market Square. Below them Narlo saw the river barges unloading at the docks. An abundance of summer produce was arriving from the warm lands to the east, south, and west; plums, guavas, and red and yellow papayas. He was glad that he would soon taste their fragrant sweetness once again.

"Why must it be us?" Cugal asked. "Why don't you get some of our own nobles, or one of the seven, to escort our guests on a tour of the city?"

"Because this is too important. These two nobles will report directly to the Lord of Kamita about what they have seen here. We must appear balanced and harmonious in our time of transition."

Narlo thought about the Mayan city of Kaminta, far to the southeast in the dense jungles. He had never been there, but he'd listened to the stories of returning missionary priests. The Lord of Kaminta had been so impressed with Xocoman commercial prowess, and the people with Xocoman religion, that the jungle city had become, even architecturally, a smaller version of its powerful neighbor to the north.

"What message does the special council want us to convey?" Narlo asked.

"Impress them with our latest cultural and economic achievements and send them home believing that the great heritage of Xocoma will continue as it has for hundreds of years."

"I wish we believed it," Cugal replied.

"Twenty-two days and still no word as to who will be the new Lord," said Narlo. "Have you heard anything, Cabran?"

"One of their servants reports to me. He claims that they fight among themselves and have agreed upon little but expanding the size of the army. That has already begun."

Narlo and Cugal looked at each other and back at Cabran the Elder.

"The Xocoman council and all the special council committees and circles stand in the way of Jaguar religious expansion. I fear that once they decide upon a new Lord, they may simply dispatch us all," Cabran the Elder said quietly. "We can't stand against an army."

"But such a move would certainly turn all of our 200,000 inhabitants against them," Cugal responded, "As well as the millions who live in our outer cities."

"I agree with Cugal," said Narlo. "They will look for other ways to gain power before resorting to open violence. My first concern is that some priests of the council may ally themselves with the seven. Who could we expect to join them?"

"Many, I'm afraid. Zadic and the five he lives with think like the Jaguar. Cakker's group, too, probably."

"Of the nine, only Zadic is proficient in the use of the powers," Cugal said.

"And even he has not perfected them," Narlo assured them. "But he does have other knowledge I would not want to fall into the hands of the seven."

"I will let you know of any new developments," said Cabran the Elder, getting up to leave. "Tomorrow at dawn the nobles of Kamita will await you at the Palace of the Owl-Butterfly. Please wear your best court attire."

Tanzel, Narlo's servant boy, helped his master dress in the predawn light. Narlo wore sandals trimmed with beads of polished jade and a pair of matching knee bracelets. A red stripe circled the bottom of his white tunic. His hair was braided, and a mantle of bloodred macaw plumes arched high above his head. A wide obsidian shoulder band pinched into both of his deeply muscled arms. In his right hand he carried the crystal rod with its handle of carved jade. Narlo stood six heads tall and was an impressive sight in his full court regalia.

"Thank you, Tanzel. Well done."

"Will you ride in a litter today?" Tanzel asked.

"I suppose."

"How I would like to experience such a thing."

"Become a priest of the First Caste and you shall."

In fact, Narlo preferred to walk, but today all the formalities must be observed in honor of their noble guests. Soon Cugal joined him on the patio. Both men were the same height and weight; when dressed identically, they might have been twins. The late-summer sky was turning from purple to crimson as they ate a breakfast of fresh fruit and corn wafers.

On a normal day, both men kept busy counseling Second Caste priests and meeting with committees on matters of state as they affected religion. As their most public duty, the thirteen priests living in the apartment compound led the sacred Sunset Ascension Ritual every seventh day at the top of the Mu Pyramid. The ritual was conducted nightly by different groups of priests of the Xocoman council.

After finishing their breakfast, both men kneeled before the temple altar in the center of the patio. They whispered the prayer of protection and guidance, and touched a finger to the earth and to the center of their foreheads. Then, standing, they bowed to the statue of Talote and left the compound.

The Palace of the Owl-Butterfly was a short distance away in Oag Pyramid Plaza. Illuminated by the first rays of the sun, the nobles from Kamita stood surrounded by an entourage of sixteen bearers and eight spear-carrying soldiers. The two wore scarlet tunics and huge necklaces inlaid with shells and human teeth to form a plumed serpent. Their mantles of tall yellow and orange feathers fanned out behind them like a glorious sunrise. The soldiers wore ornate helmets and painted leather shoulder guards. Around their necks were wide collars of polished rock, cut into many small pieces and arranged to form an elaborate mosaic. Painted leather breastplates covered their chests, and the front of their loincloths reached almost to the ground. Standing at attention by the litters were the huge bearers, who wore only red loincloths and shoulder braces. Their hair was woven into a high peak at the crown.

After introductions and a few minutes of informal conversation, Narlo, Cugal, and the Kamita noblemen stepped into their litters and were hoisted on the shoulders of the bearers. As they moved quickly through the city at a half trot, people stepped silently out of their path.

The tour began with an overview of the canal system. "Starting at the river," Narlo explained, "we dredged a network of waterways that would extend throughout the city and also connect with Lake Tepec. Thus we can easily transport trade goods, supplies, and building materials wherever they are needed. River water is also diverted into the sewer system through a separate causeway. The sewers run beneath much of the city and exit downriver." A tour of irrigated agricultural projects followed. As the visiting dignitaries looked out over the luminous green fields, Narlo wished that more of the land could be cultivated in this way. In a time of drought, he knew, it would be difficult to feed the ever-growing population.

Next Narlo commandeered an empty barge to take the group to Lake Tepec, where Cugal explained how the floating gardens provided several food crops a year. They watched fishermen setting their nets, toured the local warehouses, and observed a training camp for Xocoman soldiers. Narlo was surprised at the number of men they saw being drilled and the overall level of activity.

After returning to the city, they visited the largest of the four hundred obsidian workshops. For the first time the Kamita noblemen appeared impressed. It was obsidian products that were the chief source of Xocoma's great commercial strength, for the city's craftsmen had gained a virtual monopoly throughout the known world in the production of razors, knives, darts, and arrowheads. Locally mined obsidian was green but appeared black until held to the light. Traders also supplied the workshops with gray obsidian, which they brought from mines many days distant from Xocoma.

"We have over two hundred workshops dedicated solely to producing our exquisite, multicolored ceramics," Narlo said, wondering if he didn't sound like one of the merchants in Market Square.

Later the group visited the shops of artisans and

watched as they created jewelry, carved masks and religious figurines from jade, greenstone, and basalt inlaid with gems and shells.

The Kamitans also expressed a desire to meet the temple astronomers and astrologers, who maintained the calendar and were consulted on any decision affecting the city's destiny. This was followed by a visit to the medical building, where doctors worked with herbs, light, and vibrational sound. Finally, after a trip through the largest and finest palaces, the tour ended with a reception at the palace of Cabran the Elder, who had also invited his most trusted priests. A festive dinner was served, and Cabran spent much of the evening conversing with the visiting noblemen.

Narlo felt relieved that his part in the visit was finished, and Cugal indicated that he, too, was glad the day was over. "Did you notice that we were followed?" Cugal asked.

"Everywhere," Narlo replied.

"Who authorized the new mural—the one of the soldiers in dress uniform—on the Street of Balam-Ti?" Cugal asked.

"If I'd known it was there, I'd have picked a different route. The seven have obviously assumed control over the city's public art," Narlo said.

The dinner began with cooked-dog appetizers on little sticks, served with fermented pulque. Narlo called it the "falling-down drink." The main course consisted of deer and rabbit venison and corn cakes in sweet sap. For dessert the group was served a selection of all the fresh fruits known to man.

Narlo and Cugal walked home together along the Lord's Way, but each was alone with his thoughts about the events of the day and the increasing boldness of the seven. Torchlights burned brightly on the corner of each block. From the ceremonial fire pit at the base of the Mu Pyramid, flames leaped into the black sky as they did every night of the year. But tonight something was different. Instead of two soldiers standing at attention on each side of the stairway, there were six.

"Why a dozen men?" Narlo wondered aloud.

"Why indeed," Cugal replied.

CHAPTER SIXTEEN

"Two killing frosts and now this," Cugal said, as he stood with Narlo on the patio porch, watching the large hailstones cover the ground. The pelting roar was so loud on the roof above their heads that he looked up as if expecting the timbers to collapse under the weight of the onslaught. "Will any crops remain for the harvest festival?"

Narlo was slow to answer. "We've survived before and we will again."

The wind shifted and some of the hailstones bounced over and landed at their feet. Cugal kicked them back into the open patio.

"I've been summoned to the Palace of Government by the seven," Narlo said.

"When?" Cugal asked.

"At noon."

"Do you know why?"

"No."

"I'll go with you."

"No. They must be given no reason to suspect that you or any of the others are members of the circle," Narlo said.

The hail finally stopped, but an icy rain continued to fall in wet sheets against a black sky. Although it was only early fall, Narlo had dressed in one of his winter robes and wore an outer garment of red-dyed maguey fibers, greased to keep out the rain. His sandaled feet were soon numb with cold as he sloshed along the deserted Lord's Way. They've had forty-five days to decide, and still haven't chosen the new Lord, Narlo thought, hunching into the wind. On the wall of a temple compound he noticed another new mural. This one showed soldiers in exalted poses grouped around a central figure wearing a jaguar head. To glamorize soldiers, he thought, is against everything Xcane stood for.

Market Square was deserted. Narlo quickly scaled the stairs of Palace Square and stopped for a moment on the summit platform. The courtyard was empty and the city quiet, except for the drumming of the rain and a few barking dogs. He descended into the vast open area and walked briskly to the Palace of Government to the left of the Temple of Quetzalcoatl.

Two soldiers opened the heavy doors and he stepped into the warm, smoky room. At the far end he saw the seven sons of Xcane in thick, hooded robes, seated around a large, circular stone table. In the middle of the table was a pit filled with volcanic rocks that had been heated to a red glow and carried by runners from the lime fire pits. Standing at attention were two young scribes waiting to record the communications.

Several wood-splinter torches lighted the area, and Narlo caught the look of hatred on Khatic's face.

"Come, Atlantean. Join us," said Chquik, one of the younger sons.

"You summoned me?" Narlo asked, and bowed.

"Sit there." Chquik motioned to a bench across from the seven.

The warmth from the pit felt good to Narlo. He loosened the top ties of his coat.

"It is time that you named the other members of the Atlantean Circle," Khatic said threateningly, leaning across the table toward Narlo.

"Khatic!" Chquik snapped. "We have agreed that I will conduct this inquiry."

Khatic leaned back scowling, his forehead deeply furrowed, his eyes secretive black slits. Beneath his heavy coat Narlo fingered the serpent carved onto the jade handle of his crystal rod.

"Atlantean, it is time for you to share some information with us," Chquik said. "First, Khatic is right. The Lord must know the identity of those who sit in the Atlantean Circle."

"There is not yet a Lord," Narlo replied.

"We speak as the combined voice of the Lord," Chquik said.

"I'm sorry, but that will not do," Narlo said.

"See!" Khatic bellowed, smashing his fist on the table. "They are a subversive force that already plots against us."

"We must also study the crystal records of Xocoma," Chquik said.

"Again, I must remind you that only a member of the Atlantean Circle can time channel the records, and will do so when the Lord of Xocoma so requests or for a purpose he assigns."

"Is this true?" asked another of the brothers. "The records can only be read by one of the sixteen?"

"How would we know they speak the truth?" asked another.

"The contents of the records are already depicted in the murals of our nation for all to study and understand," Narlo said. "And you have the written collections of Lord Xcane as well."

"Not the records of your meetings, Atlantean, and not the records that explain how to use the powers," Khatic said, his anger and hatred of Narlo clearly apparent on his face, though he strove to hide them.

"Your father, the Lord of Xocoma, never asked us to reveal the records of our meetings. Had he asked, his request would have been denied. And as for the powers, like any ability, they result from years of practice."

"You dare to deny the Lord of Xocoma?" Khatic snarled, as he stood and smashed a drinking cup on the table.

"You dare to deny the sanctity of the Atlantean Circle and Xocoman council?" Narlo responded, standing to face Khatic for the second time.

"Atlantean, please sit down. Khatic, if you can't control yourself, the rest of us must ask you to leave," Chquik said.

Narlo sat down and looked at Chquik. "Will you not continue to support the Xocoman laws of your father?"

"Xocoma prospered under the guidance of our father, but that doesn't mean it can't prosper even more under our direction," Chquik said. "We don't want conflict with those you represent, but we will not allow you to place limits on the potential of our people."

Narlo took a deep breath. "Will a new Lord be announced soon?"

"Yes. Will you reconsider our requests for assistance?" Chquik asked.

"No."

"Then you are excused, Atlantean."

Narlo stood up to leave and then turned back to the table. "May I ask why murals of soldiers are being painted on the walls of the city?"

"Is that not obvious, Atlantean?" Khatic said, and laughed mockingly.

"A soldier was waiting in the prayer temple of every apartment compound in the city," the young priest explained to Narlo and Cugal as they stood in Narlo's room. The young man was soaking wet, dressed in the green and white tunic of a novice priest, his head shaved on both sides, a broad tuft of hair running from his widow's peak to his crown. Outside, the icy rain continued into the night, driving people to seek out the warmest corners of their apartments.

"Before sunset prayers the soldier read a proclamation signed by the Council of Seven, speaking as the Lord of Xocoma. It stated that the gods are angry and have unleashed the frost and crop-killing hail as punishment. It said that since the death of Xcane the priests of the Xocoman council have been lax in their attempts at appeasement. The people have the right to demand more of those who represent them to the gods."

"Was there anything more?" Cugal asked.

"No."

"How did the people respond?" Narlo asked.

"They seemed to wonder whether it might be true. They know they're going to be hungry this winter, and they'd like someone to blame.

"Frosts and hail ruin the crops every six or seven years. It's a natural cycle," Cugal said.

"People have short memories," Narlo replied.

When the young priest was gone, Cugal asked, "Would you like me to time channel from the records as you fall asleep?"

"That would be nice, my friend."

"I can use the practice."

Narlo wrapped himself in his heaviest robe and

tried to make himself comfortable as he sat on his pallet laid out on the cold floor. Cugal sat on one of the two benches that faced each other across the room and cupped his hands around a large crystal. Then he closed his eyes and began to breathe deeply. Narlo watched the flickering flame of the table lamp reflected in the facets of the crystal, but closed his eyes when Cugal began to speak.

"The energies of all that was and all that ever will be, *is.* So listen to my voice and perceive another time and another place. Draw the past into the present. Perceive a time of peace and wisdom when the people visited the chambers of light and sound and emerged balanced and energized. Draw the images closer and closer until you are one with the energy and you release and can rest."

The impressions, at first faint and fantasylike, became more and more vivid, until Narlo was walking in the green hills above a white Atlantean city. Wearing a golden toga and sandals, he made his way down out of the hills and into a beautiful outdoor garden filled with smiling, happy people. A woman played a harp. A white-haired man sat on the edge of a carved fountain, speaking to a large group of people who were relaxing in the grass at his feet.

Narlo knew the man was talking about divine order, and moved close enough to hear his words. "All is as it should be. There are no accidents. Your energy is expressed in your emotions, your thoughts, your words, and your acts. These then manifest the experiences you require to forgive yourself and bring your soul into balance. So it follows that the collective emotions, thoughts, words, and acts of our people create the environment we must all experience. If the majority focus their energy upon love and harmony, we will have love and harmony. If the majority focus their energy upon possessions and power, we will have conflict and strife. If the majority focus their thoughts upon fear and blood, we will have devastation. We are all *one,* and the dominant values of our people will manifest to influence everyone."

Narlo awakened to the crackling sound of lightning striking nearby. It was followed by an earthshaking boom as thunder rumbled slowly across the valley and echoed off the distant mountains. The lamp was out. Cugal was gone. Alone in the darkness, Narlo listened to the rain lashing the roof. He prayed for guidance.

CHAPTER SEVENTEEN

Golden leaves fell throughout the valley and blew across the streets of Xocoma, gathering in piles at the edges of the palaces, temples, and pyramids on the Lord's Way. From the top of the Mu Pyramid stairs, Narlo watched as the late-afternoon sun reflected off the gleaming walls and statuary, bathing the great city in a glow as brilliant as the falling leaves.

In the distance Narlo could see large groups of farmers returning from the fields. The canals were filled with barges moving slowly toward Lake Tepec or floating downriver. Some were empty and would return fully loaded at the rising of the sun. Others were on their way to distant lands, carrying the products that assured Xocoma the prosperity and power that other nations secured with their armies.

"Do you ever wonder what will happen if the seven combine the power of a strong army with the weight of our commercial dominance?" Cugal said, joining his friend. His servant boy was attempting to dress him for the evening Sunset Ascension Ritual, but Cugal wouldn't stand still.

"A strong army is one thing," Narlo said, still

staring off into the distance. "But a Jaguar army fueled by human sacrifice is another."

"Our religion wouldn't allow such a—" Cugal's servant boy spoke before realizing that he shouldn't have. He hurried away, ashamed.

"Cooperation is impossible, isn't it?" Cugal said.

"Yes. We know it and they know it."

"Do you expect them to take any action at the Harvest Festival next week?"

"I'd love to run a scan line on one of the seven. But I doubt that I'll get close enough."

Narlo and Cugal took turns leading the ascension ritual, but tonight it was Narlo's turn and it was he who wore the jade mask and scarlet feathered headdress. His robe was designed to resemble a sunset and was fashioned from intricately woven bird feathers, beginning at his neck with the reds of cardinals and macaws, then shading into the yellow of toucans and the black of crows.

As the sun's edge touched the far horizon, Narlo stepped in front of the flaming fire pit at the top of the stairs. From here he appeared as a figure in the fire to the thousands of people below on the Lord's Way and to those who watched from a distance—from their apartment patios and from the surrounding streets and fields. Next, a procession of white-robed priests emerged on both sides of the pyramid and slowly descended the stairway. The last man stopped twenty steps below Narlo, another twenty steps farther down, and so on until a priest was standing on every twentieth step and the rows had fanned out across the face of the pyramid. From these positions they would repeat the words of the ritual as Narlo spoke them, until the syllables became an echoing mantra that those lining the Lord's Way could hear. Most of the watchers knew the ritual by heart and joined in the solemn chant.

Torchlights danced in the twilight. The conch trumpets sounded, sending forth the proper vibrations from the four corners of the pyramid. Muted drumming followed, blending with the soft sounds of whistles and clay flutes. The people in the streets closed their eyes and began to hum the "ohm," at first softly, then in harmonious waves that filled the city with the holy sound. Tired from the day's work but inspired by their faith, they joined hands and swayed back and forth to the rhythm that reached deeply into their souls and flowed up through the seven energy centers.

"In the divine name of the Giver of All Life, I open to the light." As Narlo raised both hands in the air and spoke the words, they were echoed by the priests and quickly reached the swaying people below. "I offer my body, my mind, and my spirit to the light. Let thy divine will and mine be as one. Give us the strength to release our fears, to share the light and serve our people."

Throughout the ritual the people continued to chant the "ohm" and sway as one. Then, as the ceremony drew to a close and Narlo spun the circle of fire that symbolized the all-encompassing Talote, those on the Lord's Way opened their eyes and began to chant, "We seek the light of the Giver of Life. We seek the light of the Giver of Life." Silently the priests moved back up the stairway as the sky faded from crimson to blue-black and stars blanketed the heavens. Just as quietly the people let go of each other's hands and returned to their homes.

Following the opening ceremonies of the fifty-two member Xocoman council, Cabran the Elder rose and stepped to the speaker's platform in the Palace of Prayer. "The Harvest Festival begins in two days. You are all familiar with your duties. The crop failures mean we will have a more difficult task than we have had for many years. The seven have claimed that the fault is ours, and some believe them. The seven have also formally requested that Zadic perform the opening ceremonies."

Cabran the Elder sat down to open the forum for discussion. One priest rose, and the old man signaled for him to speak.

"The Harvest Festival is a religious occasion. The seven have nothing to do with it. The Elder of the Xocoman council has always officiated at the opening ceremonies."

Narlo glanced across the hall at Zadic, sitting smugly with his supporters. He had a narrow face, tiny black eyes, and his top front teeth were missing.

Cakkers was the next to speak. "In a time of transition we should cooperate with the government. What does it matter?"

"It matters!" Narlo exclaimed, in a voice so loud it startled those who were watching Cakkers. "The seven need a priest to serve as their instrument as they work to abolish our council and replace our religion with that of the Jaguar."

"I don't think we can assume—" Cakkers sputtered.

"Oh yes, we can! It's obvious from the pronouncement of blame. It's obvious from the new murals being painted on the walls of this city. They need a priest who thirsts for power. Someone they can control," Narlo said, staring intently at Zadic.

Now Zadic rose, his face flushed with anger. "The Atlantean is a fool. He has always been a troublemaker. Every member of this council knows that."

"The members of this council know exactly who

and what I am. They also know you, Zadic. I call for an immediate vote. How many agree?"

All present raised their hands except for Zadic and Cakkers and six of their supporters.

"How many of the Xocoman council want Cabran the Elder to conduct the opening ceremonies of the Harvest Festival?" Narlo demanded in his most commanding voice, raising his hand as he spoke.

Forty-three priests raised their hands. Cabran the Elder did not vote. "And so it is," Narlo declared.

Tens of thousands of people from the outlands journeyed to Xocoma to attend the many religious festivals held each year. They came to visit the shrines, enjoy the festivities, and marvel at the wealth of goods offered for sale in Market Square and in the many outlying trade centers that had been opened to serve the festivalgoers. Everyone dressed in costumes to match the occasion, and the dancing and singing lasted until the moon was high in the sky.

On the morning of the Harvest Festival, Zadic walked slowly down the steps of the Oag Pyramid to light the Three-Day Fire of Faith, officially opening the festivities. Thousands had crowded into the plaza, and thousands more stood in the streets outside. After finishing the opening incantations, Zadic looked out at the sea of faces before him and said, "I regret to inform all of you of the death of Cabran the Elder, Master Speaker of the Xocoman council, who has opened this festival for longer than most of us can remember. The seven sons of Xcane, speaking as the Lord of Xocoma, and the fifty-one members of the Xocoman council, ask that this festival be dedicated to the memory of our departed leader, who peacefully joined Talote last night while he slept."

Narlo listened in disbelief as he stood with Cugal in the long line of formally attired priests on the first tier of the pyramid. "They've murdered him!" he cried, his muscles tensed and his breath coming in short bursts. Cugal grasped Narlo's arm in a show of support.

Zadic continued, "Our gods are angry. They've taken your crops and your religious leader from you, and they will take even more unless they are appeased."

As he spoke, a row of fully armed soldiers marched into the plaza and took up positions behind the priests. Narlo looked at Cugal and then turned to face a soldier standing behind him. The sullen-faced man drew an obsidian knife and held it poised. He looked Narlo straight in the eyes.

"Don't!" Cugal whispered, tightening his grip on Narlo's arm. "He'd kill you before you could use the powers."

Narlo tried to focus on Zadic's voice, but his mind was swirling with stratagems for dealing with the traitor priest and the seven . . . until the soldiers carried the limp, drugged body of a dark-haired young woman up the steps to the altar. Then he quickly returned to the scene before him. He felt the sharp blade of the knife resting against his back, and he felt Zadic's words slice through his mind and tear at his soul.

"Our gods have given and given to the people of Xocoma. Now it's time that we give something in return. What more perfect offering can we make to them than the most beautiful life among us? Our gods give us life. We give them life."

The music began. Unseen voices chanted, "Our gods give us life. We give them life," and some of the crowd joined in the chant. "Our gods give us life. We give them life." Many visitors to the city found nothing unusual in the ceremony, for it was a common practice in their home lands.

Zadic was wearing the head of a spotted jaguar as he called on the old gods by name. "To Garr, flayed god of fertility. To Kann, fire god of life and death. To Kitz, water god of heaven and earth." Tears streamed down Narlo's cheeks as Zadic raised the sacrificial knife and plunged it into the senseless body on the altar.

CHAPTER EIGHTEEN

"With my six brothers at my side as the Lord's Elders, I vow to lead Xocoma to its greatest glory," said Khatic as he was proclaimed Lord of Xocoma on the last day of the Harvest Festival. He wore the jaguar mantle, a spotted jaguar pelt cape, and the uniform of an army officer.

Thousands gathered in Palace Square and on the surrounding summit platform, straining to hear the blustering, long-winded speech.

Narlo was not there. Cugal carried the news to his friend, who was at Nlers's study on the Street of Zaquicaz.

"It was as we expected," Nlers said. "Khatic managed to gain control of the army. The brothers probably had no choice."

"What do we do now?" Cugal asked.

"What can we do but guide the people for as long as possible? The Xocoman council has their ears, but the soldiers can also use individual temples to proclaim the message of the Jaguar. If Khatic can enlist public opinion to overthrow the council, he'll be a hero instead of a betrayer," Narlo said.

"It's time to start hiding the records," Cugal declared.

"What knowledge does Zadic have that he can offer the seven?" Nlers asked.

"The techniques of mental projection. We can expect the dark priests to use these powers. Only the Atlantean Circle shares the mind connection and knowledge of the scan line. And unless they can find the crystal panels and coerce one of our circle to read them, the sacred records as well as the Atlantean records are safe."

The smell of burning fire pits wafted up from beyond the apartment walls as Narlo walked through crunching leaves, along the narrow alley that led to the apartment compound he shared with his fellow priests. Three soldiers followed him openly now, and Narlo knew they would wait outside the walls until he returned. Behind a small cabinet in the basement of the compound was a stairway leading down into the cave that was the meeting place of the Atlantean Circle. It was dark in the cavern, and Narlo was glad to feel its comforting warmth envelop him as he made his way along the passage to his friends, waiting for him up ahead.

After performing the opening rituals, Narlo spoke to the fifteen robed and hooded figures sitting around the circle. "For those of you who were not there today, we elected Xrote the Elder to be Master Speaker of the Xocoman council. We also voted on seven Second Caste priests to replace Zadic and Cakkers and most of their supporters, who have resigned."

"Most of their supporters?" someone said.

"They left one priest to report on our activities, and we have no power to remove him."

"What of the new religious council?" someone asked.

"You know as much about it as I do," Narlo said. "Khatic has created a Religious Council of the Jaguar, headed by Zadic. I know they've recruited several Second Caste priests to join them."

"Eventually, Khatic will use it to replace the Xocoman council," someone said.

"He'll try," Narlo answered.

"What do we do now?" Xpico asked. "I have already hidden my own records."

"So have I," said another member.

"Twice I have tried, unsuccessfully, to get the Xocoman council to take a public stand against the Cult of the Jaguar and the practice of human sacrifice," Narlo reminded them.

"They're afraid," said Cugal. "They feel everybody in Xocoma already knows we stand against the Jaguar practices. To make it an issue could bring down the wrath of Khatic's army."

"There were more sacrifices today in Oag Plaza," someone reported.

"They were supposedly a band of Zapotecs who were attempting to rob a Xocoman barge."

"Do you believe that?"

Narlo raised his hand. "I think we should all maintain our mental connection from now on. And we should increase our efforts to combat the ideas of the Jaguar. We can enter the temple compounds and speak to our people. If all sixteen of us speak to one group a day, in thirty days we'll have talked to 480 groups."

"Remind them of the oneness," Cugal said. "Be sure they understand that if the thinking of the majority shifts to fear, we're all doomed."

"Is it advisable to demonstrate some of the mental powers to get their attention?" Alita asked.

"If that's what it takes," Narlo said.

* * *

"The Jaguar Council has fifty-two members and meets weekly on the day of Xhat in the Eastern Palace at Oag Plaza," Alita said. "Seven of the finest artists in Xocoma have been drafted to repaint the murals."

Wrapped in his rabbit coat, Narlo sat in the compound's temple, searching for ways to combat the jaguar influence. Alita sat beside him. Cugal was pacing up and down on the other side of the warming fire, which crackled when Narlo dropped another log on the hot coals. Outside, a few fragile snowflakes floated down through the patio.

"Do I need to ask the subject of the murals?" Narlo said.

"No."

"I do," Cugal said.

"A row of jaguars, each grasping a human heart in his claws. They circle the entire base of the inner temple." Alita slowly traced the red stripe down her face with her index finger as she spoke. "There's something else." Narlo looked over at her, and Cugal stopped pacing. "In today's public ritual at Oag Plaza, Zadic asked those who accept the Jaguar religion to paint their apartments red, 'so the gods will know who to favor.'"

"What?" Narlo and Cugal asked in unison.

"Khatic envisions painting our white city red," Alita explained. "The Palace of the Lord has already been repainted."

"Bloodred," Narlo said. "Intimidation by color." He threw his writing stick into the fire. Red sparks leaped into the air and disappeared.

"You must accept what is, Narlo," Cugal said gently.

"I won't accept a Xocoma painted bloodred as a symbol of sacrifice."

"You're a priest, not a soldier, Narlo. Lately I think you forget that."

173

"Maybe for the better," Narlo said as he stood and walked through the open doorway into the patio. When he reached his own room, he lifted the jade and crystal rod from a shelf and took his rabbitskin hat from a storage box.

The Lord's Way was nearly empty and snow was beginning to accumulate along the steps of the palaces and temples. Narlo leaned into the wind, breathing deeply and drawing his psychic energy up through the centers. The Oag Pyramid seemed to loom more ominously than ever as he reached the Eastern Palace.

Four soldiers stood outside the doors, spears ready. Without hesitating, Narlo ascended the stairs and took out the crystal rod. He projected more energy than necessary, for the soldiers flew back against the wall. Two fell to the floor unconscious and another fell but scrambled to his feet and ran. The other backed away slowly.

Narlo grasped the immense handle of the carved wooden door and yanked it open. In the torchlit room sat a circle of black-robed figures. Thirteen.

"Where is Zadic?" Narlo shouted.

"Get out, Atlantean," someone screamed.

The dark figures rose as one. His eyes flashing furiously, Narlo raised his crystal rod and then lowered it until it was pointing at the dark figures in front of him. As he projected his energies through it, the priests were already summoning their own powers, and the clashing energy shot through the room like crazed lightning. Then the dark figures were pushed back.

"Where is Zadic?"

"He's not here," someone said.

Narlo knew these were young priests whose powers were not yet fully developed, for their combined mental energy was no match for his own.

"Thirteen. This is a sending circle," shouted Narlo

accusingly, looking at the man closest to him. He was young and he stared back at Narlo, terrified.

"What are you sending?" Narlo demanded.

But the young priest didn't answer, so Narlo projected more energy, pushing him back against the wall until his features began to twist and flatten.

"What?"

"Just . . . just . . . just the message," the priest stammered.

Narlo sent out more energy. The other twelve priests stood frozen.

"What is the message?"

"The Jaguar will save you."

"Directed where?"

"To the apartments in the thirty-second quadrant."

"How often? To whom?"

"Ten quadrants. Every day."

Narlo tipped the rod to the sky, and the priest standing next to him collapsed on the floor. The others did not move, but a look of relief flashed across their faces.

"Where is Zadic?" Narlo asked another priest.

"At his apartment or with the Lord of Xocoma. I don't know."

As Narlo backed through the still open door, a dozen spear-carrying soldiers ran down the street toward the palace. Then he ducked behind the frontal pillars and raced down the side stairs, which lead to an alley. Soon he was on the Street of Xe, running toward Zadic's apartment compound. *You are a priest, Narlo. Act like a priest!* He was still repeating the words to himself when he entered Zadic's apartment.

"What took you so long, Atlantean?" Zadic cackled from the depths of a corridor.

Narlo spun to his right to see three soldiers emerge from one doorway and Zadic from another.

"Don't," Zadic said, raising his own crystal rod. "I'm sure we are quite well matched, so you would be wasting your energy. Besides, you're outnumbered."

Cakkers and four others stepped from the shadows behind Zadic.

"I'm willing to talk," Zadic said. "If that's what you had in mind. Or was it hand-to-hand combat?"

"Talk," Narlo said, lowering his rod and slipping it into the pocket of his coat.

"Follow me," Zadic directed, and led the way down the corridor. Narlo followed. They continued on past the communal bath, past the temple patio and down a hallway to Zadic's meeting room. A warming pit glowed in the middle of a table, which was surrounded by eight chairs. Zadic motioned Narlo to sit down and closed the door so they would be alone, although Narlo sensed others in the next room.

"Competition is good for business, Atlantean," Zadic hissed through the gaps in his teeth.

"You intend to paint Xocoma red?"

"Khatic sees it as a way of keeping score."

"It's not quite that simple, Zadic."

"Yes it is, Atlantean. You wish that it was not, but it is really quite simple."

"Then simplify it even more, Zadic. What does Khatic offer?"

"Nothing. There is no need."

Narlo didn't reply.

"We'll beat you, Atlantean, without lifting a spear." He laughed. "Only Khatic would like you dead. Myself, my associates and the six brothers would prefer to see you discredited. We wish the people to view you as a traitor."

Zadic's words seemed to penetrate Narlo's brain like poisoned arrows, so that for a few moments he couldn't think. "Even if you destroy the Xocoman council, you know that your bloody sacrifices won't change the weather or grow more crops. How will you explain such problems when you're in control?"

Zadic pushed himself away from the table and held both his hands toward the warming pit. "You are too naive, Atlantean. The people know their dark thoughts and wrong deeds. They already know they are guilty. The fault is always theirs, just as you say it is when you explain your foolish ideas of rebirth and balancing the soul records."

Narlo looked deeply into Zadic's tiny eyes. He didn't speak.

"You frighten the people with your talk of self-responsibility. I frighten them with the threat of angry gods. What's the difference?"

"Self-responsibility isn't fear."

Zadic laughed so hard he began to cough, and summoned a servant to bring him something to drink. When it arrived, Narlo smelled the pungent odor of pulque.

"Fear of self-responsibility may be the ultimate fear, Atlantean. People would rather blame others for their circumstances than bear the blame themselves. That is why we will easily win."

"Then why does Khatic need an army?"

"Why do you insist on making things harder for yourself and those who follow you? For two moon cycles your priests have taught nightly in the apartment compounds. Those accepting the Atlantean teachings are marked."

"Or saved," Narlo said.

"Saved? For what? A better life next time? Maybe they hope to follow in the footsteps of a priest who talks of light and love but acts with the intent of a soldier in battle?"

Narlo felt a shame that exploded into anger. He stood and reached across the table, grabbing Zadic's scrawny neck. The priest's eyes widened in terror and his screech drew a storm of men into the room. A rope net dropped over Narlo from the dark recesses of the ceiling and he was at the mercy of his captors.

Zadic stood up, brushed himself off, and stared down at his rival, who lay pinned beneath the net and surrounded by soldiers.

"You see how much alike we are, Atlantean? You just chose the wrong side," Zadic told him, grasping his throat with one hand and gesturing toward the door with the other. "Throw the traitor out."

The soldiers dragged Narlo, still netted, through the rooms and corridors of the apartment, to the front entrance. There they removed the ropes and threw him down the stairs into the gathering snow.

CHAPTER NINETEEN

It was one of the first warm evenings of early spring, and the people of the artisan apartment compound were shocked to see the Atlantean standing in ritual attire at their temple altar. Forty-seven people lived in the compound, and most of them crowded into the patio to listen.

"On whose authority do you speak here?" shouted a soldier, striding into the patio.

"As a member of the Xocoman council I am the authority on all matters of religion," Narlo said. Throughout the winter he had spoken in the patios of Xocoma, but this was the first time he had been challenged by a soldier.

"I think not," said the man, raising his spear threateningly. Two more soldiers rushed into the patio to join him.

Murmurs of fear spread through the watching throng.

"Leave," the soldier said, motioning to his comrades to escort Narlo from the altar.

As the men approached, Narlo raised his jade and crystal rod. Without hesitating, the soldiers marched straight toward the Atlantean until they encountered the full force of his projected energy. Then, as if struck by a giant unseen hand, the two men flew backward and landed in a heap on the patio floor. One of their spears rolled away, and someone in the crowd quickly snatched it from sight.

Narlo directed the rod at the standing soldier. "Now *you* leave," he said quietly.

There was a spontaneous burst of applause as the three uniformed men hurried out the door of the compound. Then the crowd turned to Narlo in anticipation.

"I'm sorry you had to see that," Narlo said. "But the Jaguar is afraid, and the Jaguar wants you to be afraid of its vengeful gods. For years you've listened to my words, both directly and indirectly, through your temple priest. You know I speak to you of love, not fear. You know I seek to maintain the peace and prosperity we've always known.

"So let us dismiss fear. What you mentally sow you will harvest. Sow the seeds of love. Dwell upon your blessings, not what is lacking. Accept that you are the creator of this life as you are the creator of every life."

The people listened in rapt attention as Narlo shared the wisdom that had been handed down from the days of Atlantis. "But how do we ignore the soldiers that are everywhere in greater numbers?" asked an old woman. Her husband stood beside her, holding her hand.

"If you resist them, you will draw them into your life."

"But you just resisted the soldiers."

"It was the only way I could get to speak with you. They were already confronting me, and the day may come when they will confront you, too, and force you to take a stand. But until then do not react mentally or physically to their presence or actions. Instead, mentally send them love. It will confuse them and cause them to question what they do.

"And remember that when two or more of you are gathered for a shared purpose, your combined energy is doubled, tripled, quadrupled, or more. So join your energies for the love of God whom we call Talote, whose divinity is expressed in the 'ohm.' Talote is you and you are he, as the one believes so shall it be."

Then the ohming and chanting began. "Talote is you and you are he, as the one believes so shall it be. Talote is you and you are he, as the one believes so shall it be." Standing at the altar, his hands raised and his eyes closed, Narlo felt strangely at peace, yet resigned.

The Atlantean led a group prayer to Talote to put an end to the dry weather. There had been little snow last winter and no rain this spring. The service lasted until after sunset, and many people stayed to visit with Narlo in the torchlit patio. When the last question was finally answered and he was preparing to leave, a young woman stepped from the shadows.

"Stay," she said. She was tall and slender, with firm breasts and slim hips, and she was dressed in a short overblouse and long skirt. There was both delicacy and strength in her face, and her eyes revealed her intelligence and independent spirit. Her long, dark hair glistened in the torchlight.

"I really can't—" Narlo began, about to excuse himself.

"Yes, you can," she said, taking his hand. She smiled and looked deeply into his eyes. "My name is Leeva. Come."

Holding Narlo's hand, she led him through a corridor, stopping to light a fire lamp from a wood splinter torch, then into her room—an artist's room. The walls were painted from floor to ceiling with a mural depicting men and women dancing, singing, and resting beneath green trees filled with colorful birds. Hanging on hooks painted to look like tree branches were beautiful necklaces, ornate combs and armbands. Leeva set the lamp on a table made of several carved wooden boxes. There were two chairs in the room, and along the outside wall was a bed covered with a blanket. Woven into the center of the blanket was the sacred symbol.

Narlo removed his feathered mantle as Leeva untied his tunic, then knelt to remove his sandals. As she stood, she let her skirt drop to the floor. Gently Narlo lifted her blouse over her head and drew her into his arms. They kissed long and passionately, until Narlo lifted Leeva and carried her to the bed. They said nothing, even as they merged into one. When the lamp flickered out, they continued their lovemaking in the darkness.

Narlo recalled for a moment his mind connection with the others of the Atlantean Circle. If they were awake, they might be experiencing mentally what he was feeling physically. He smiled at the idea and turned again to the beautiful young woman beneath him.

When they were done, Narlo held her in his arms and stroked her hair. "Thank you," he whispered.

"Thank you," she replied.

Then they talked of many things—of their work and the darkness that was descending upon their city. They talked about a young woman who had lived in the apartment but had recently disappeared. They talked about food and other pleasures, and the beautiful fabrics that filled Market Square.

"I've heard that priests make love to other priests," said Leeva.

"I've heard that artisans make the most inspiring lovers," Narlo replied.

"Is it true?"

He hugged her tighter and smiled, but it was too dark for her to see.

The full moon was high in the sky when Narlo stepped out the door of the compound patio. Three soldiers standing on the other side of the street cast long shadows that snaked across the mortar and ended at Narlo's feet. Narlo smiled at the men, and breathed deeply of the good smells of damp earth and blossoming trees as he tied his coat at the neck. Then, his feathered mantle under his arm, he set off at a brisk pace up the narrow Street of the Owls, the soldiers following twenty paces behind.

At the wider Street of Jewels, he turned right and walked past blocks of wall murals painted by the artisans who lived inside the apartment complexes. There were no soldiers to be seen in these paintings. Instead, they showed Talote, Quetzalcoatl, and Xocoman priests amid religious celebrations. In others, people could be seen creating paintings, sculpture, and jewelry. Farther on, a weaver was pictured at his loom, preparing a carpet to decorate the House of the Lord. Everywhere was the sacred symbol.

Narlo found himself envying the simple life of the artisans. They lived in crowded compounds, and they received wages only slightly higher than those who farmed the fields, but they spent their days expressing their love of beauty and sharing their talents with other Xocomans. He recalled the joy of making love to Leeva, and the pleasure he felt just talking to her. This is not a time to become involved, he thought, knowing he could bring her harm, and Khatic could use her against him.

The soldiers matched Narlo's pace and maintained

their distance. Under his coat Narlo tightened his grip on the jade and crystal rod and focused on maintaining a high level of psychic energy. He crossed the Street of Balam-Ti and was entering a narrow alley when they struck. Momentarily distracted by the sound of barking dogs, Narlo didn't sense the coming attack or hear the soldiers footsteps as they broke into a run. When he turned, a spear shaft smashed into the side of his head, hurling him against a wall. He felt dizzy, and his feet collapsed beneath him as he drew the rod from the pocket of his coat. But a soldier kicked his arm and the rod hit the wall, shattering the crystal. Narlo heard the jade handle clatter to the street and roll away as another pole slammed against his back, throwing him face down in the street.

Cugal! Narlo called out silently, with all the mental force he could muster.

The soldiers were snarling obscenities as they kicked at him. Narlo rolled backward and was almost to his feet when the biggest man kicked him in the groin. His tortured scream sliced through the night, piercing the dreams of those asleep beyond the alley walls. Then the scream faded as he gasped for breath, for his very life. He was still gasping for enough air to fill his lungs when one of the soldiers growled at him.

"You're through talking to the people." Narlo opened his eyes far enough to see the man pull his knife from its scabbard. The other two wrenched him into an upright position while a third man grabbed Narlo's hair and yanked his head straight back. Something was inserted between his teeth and then twisted, forcing his mouth open. A hook was slipped over his lower jaw, cutting through the bottom of his mouth and piercing his chin. Narlo felt the blood run down his neck and onto his chest.

Above him he could barely make out a pair of hazy moons and swirling shadows edged with pain and fear. Someone was attempting to grab his slippery tongue. *They're going to cut out my tongue*, he thought. *They're going to cut out my tongue*. The darkness was closing in when he heard the sound of running feet and many men shouting. He recognized Cugal's voice and then lost consciousness.

CHAPTER TWENTY

Narlo awakened to feel a wet cloth swabbing his forehead. His eyes darted fearfully around the room until they focused on Cugal's smiling face.

"You're all right, Narlo. You're all right."

Narlo took a shuddering breath that ripped at his insides and made him tremble with pain. He closed his eyes and breathed in shallow, short gasps. As the memory of the encounter flooded his mind, he ran his tongue along the roof of his mouth and sighed in relief.

"I heard you calling to me in my sleep," Cugal said. "The soldiers ran when they saw us."

Narlo tried to talk, but the dark waves rolled over him, pushing and pulling him back and forth between the lands of life and death. Not a word escaped his mouth. But in the stillness his boyhood reached out and lured him back to play the games of youth. His father was there, too, encouraging him, showing him how to use his stick, to hit the ball as it bounced down the court. His mother was calling him home to eat.

When he awoke again, Nlers was standing beside him, along with several others. Narlo heard them talking, and realized they were upset about something the soldiers had delivered.

"From the Oag Plaza sacrifice?"

"It's a heart."

"But why bring it here?"

"I've asked all the other priests. No one here knows an artisan woman named Leeva."

"Maybe Narlo did."

Narlo tried to scream beneath the drowning dark waves. He could see Leeva's face glowing in the blackness. Running his hand through her hair, which became his mother's hair, and they cried together. Crying when his father died. Crying at his cremation. Crying at his mother's cremation. Crying together, all four of them, in a field of yellow flowers. And then Leeva was laughing and speaking to him. "It doesn't matter. I'm not gone. See me. Touch me." Narlo looked again into her eyes and saw her gentleness, her courage. She was on the verge of tears but she smiled a lovely, distant smile as she gazed at things he couldn't see.

"I'm not gone, Narlo," said his mother.

"I'm not gone, Narlo," said his father. "Life continues, just as you teach. No one dies."

"I want to stay here," Narlo said.

"When it's time, Atlantean, when it's time." The three of them were laughing as they walked away. Narlo ran after them, plunging through a field of flowers that grew deeper and deeper until he could hardly see above the cloud of yellow blossoms. *"Wait for me. Wait for me."* But the three had reached the edge of the meadow and were climbing through the trees to the far ridge. By the time he reached the ridge it was too dark to see where they had gone. He wandered in the darkness for what seemed like a very long time. Then it grew light again, and he realized he was calling Cugal's name as he slowly opened his eyes.

He was lying on a bed, in his own room, at his own apartment. When he tried to move, his head swam and every bone in his body screamed in pain. Young Tanzel was sitting at the foot of the bed, patiently awaiting his master's return from the world of dreams.

Cugal appeared in the doorway, an anxious look on his face. Narlo asked for water.

"You've been unconscious for three days," Cugal told him.

"Many priests worked in shifts to heal you," Tanzel said.

"The healers say you must lie still for a while or your head will not heal," Cugal continued.

"Tell me of Leeva," said Narlo.

"How did you know?"

"Tell me."

"Soldiers tied and beat several people in the artisans' compound to learn whom you had stayed with. They captured Leeva at her working place, where she proudly confessed to spending the night with you and spit on the soldiers."

For four days the healers came to massage Narlo's body and send him healing energy through their hands. When he was strong enough to sit up, Nlers, Xpico, and others of the Xocoman council and Atlantean Circle came to talk with him and to plan.

"You must disappear, vanish underground," Cugal said over and over again.

"Not yet. But I won't go out alone again."

"It is getting worse by the day," Nlers told him. "There's still no rain, and again Khatic lays the blame for the drought at the council's feet."

"What do the people think?"

"As many believe him as don't. But the Jaguar isn't so sure of winning or they wouldn't have tried to silence you, Narlo."

Xpico sat on the edge of Narlo's bed and began to send energy into his legs.

"Here, I brought you something," Nlers said, handing Narlo a package wrapped in cotton that had been dyed with bright colors.

Narlo unwrapped the carved jade rod, refitted with a perfect crystal. "One of your priests found it in the street the night you were beaten. This crystal may be even more powerful than the first one."

"Thank you, Nlers," Narlo said, and the two men embraced.

"I want to conduct the ascension ritual tonight," Narlo announced. He had been standing up and walking around the apartment compound for five days, slowly regaining his strength.

"You're still not strong enough to climb the stairs of the Mu Pyramid," Cugal said. "And you are definitely not ready to face the people's animosity. I've had people spit on me in the streets."

"I'll learn many things if I conduct the ritual, Cugal. Please, help me."

Narlo, wearing only a white robe instead of his heavy ritual attire, stood and gazed weakly into the fire as it leaped into the warm evening sky. At the bottom of the long flight of stairs stood the people of Xocoma—thousands of them. In the distance the sun was about to touch the horizon. The white-robed priests marched out along both sides of the platform and descended the stairs.

As always, the torchlights danced in the twilight along the Lord's Way. The conch trumpets sounded from the four corners, followed by gentle music. But the people did not respond. There was no "ohm," no swaying. Only thousands of solemn faces looking up at the Atlantean.

"In the divine name of the Giver of All Life, I open to the light." Narlo raised both hands in the air as he spoke the words. "I offer my body, my mind, and my spirit to the light. Let thy divine—"

"Nooooo," cried the people. "Nooooo!"

Narlo stopped in disbelief. Angry shouts split the night, rumbling through the city and battering his mind. He trembled. Then, as if on cue, the people began storming up the stairs of the pyramid. Running. Knocking the priests aside or throwing them off the stairs. Those stationed higher up the pyramid ran for their lives, racing up the steps ahead of the murderous horde.

"Cugal," Narlo called out. His friend was immediately by his side.

Narlo pulled his crystal rod from his robe, and Cugal drew his own crystal. Then they nodded to each other and braced themselves.

The angry crowd had almost overtaken the priests that were scurrying toward the summit. Stepping forward, Narlo and Cugal moved to the center of the stairway and raised their crystals.

"Back! Back! Back!" Their projected energies clashed with the advancing throng about twelve steps from the top of the pyramid. The first people to hit the invisible wall were thrown off their feet. Two were pushed off the stairs and slid all the way down the steep, polished pyramid to the next tier. Probably to their death, Narlo thought sadly as he forced himself to focus on the projection. Unless he and Cugal were successful, he had no doubt the mob would throw every one of the priests off the top of the pyramid.

"Back! Back! Back!" Both crystals were glowing and pulsing an iridescent blue. Narlo looked into the eyes of the people and sensed their fear and frustration. He knew they needed someone to blame for the drought and what it would do to their lives. They needed to act so they could feel in control of their destiny, if only for a moment. He knew they had listened to the Jaguar and would not listen to reason. Not now. Now, they wanted blood.

The people on the stairs below were shoving those in front of them, trying to force their way up the stairs. Those at the front were being crushed against the force field. Soon more were forced off the stairs. Several tried to slide down the face of the pyramid to escape the crush.

Narlo felt the mental energy surging through him, but for a moment his body grew weaker and he thought he might faint. Cugal saw his friend falter and put his free hand around Narlo's waist. With Cugal's support and great force of will, he managed to stand firm and held his arm high, projecting enough energy to hold back the crowd.

The sky had faded from crimson to blue and then black before the people gave up and the last of them descended the stairs. The safety of the priests assured, Narlo collapsed. Cugal carried him to a comfortable pallet, where his white-robed associates began to send him energy and healing through the laying on of hands.

Cugal stood guard at the top of the stairs and watched as the last of the angry mob dispersed. Several broken bodies lay crumpled on the tiers. The crescent moon had arched a quarter of the way into the sky before Narlo regained consciousness. He stood up and thanked each priest personally.

"Those who attacked us were but a few of those in attendance," Cugal said.

"But there were more in the crowd against us than for us," Narlo reminded him.

"It could have been arranged."

"Or the result of one of Zadic's mind programs."

As the priests slowly descended the pyramid stairs,

they noticed a Pheladian flying ship appear on the horizon behind the Oag Pyramid, then slowly drop down through the night sky. As it flew along the Lord's Way, level with the Mu Pyramid, the familiar whirring sound and spiraling lights filled Narlo with a sense of hope. He and the others watched as the ship landed quietly in Palace Square.

CHAPTER TWENTY-ONE

"The Pheladians will take the crystal records with them," Nlers explained to Narlo as the two men shared breakfast on the Atlantean's apartment patio. "The people who remain loyal to us are all hiding their records. I've duplicated those I feel we might need, and have hidden them in the caves."

Narlo committed the secret location to memory. Endless miles of volcanic tunnels existed under the valley surface. It was easy to hide things in the caves so that they would never be found.

"Will the Pheladians take any of the Wise Ones with them?" Narlo asked.

"Those desiring to go."

The Atlantean nodded. "And they can't help us?"

"They can only observe. Xocoma was the one surviving, successful example of Pheladian concepts applied to this world. They know the shortages resulting from the crop failures can be corrected with increased trade. But Khatic wants the people to suffer until they beg him to save them."

"And all they have to do to be saved is get rid of their ineffectual priests, welcome the Jaguar's army, and accept his fear-based religion."

"Cugal is right. It's time for all of you to go underground."

"What about you, Nlers? They know you keep records."

"Khatic would do nothing that might anger the Pheladians until he knows for sure they won't interfere. Everyone has heard stories of the flying ship's terrible powers."

Cugal entered the patio and joined his two friends at the table. His hair was unbraided and he wore the clothes of a merchant. "I've been visiting the compounds of the artisans," he said. "Khatic has commanded them to create huge statues of the old gods—Garr, Kann, and Kitz." Cugal motioned to his servant boy to bring him lunch and a drink. "That's not the worst of it. A new altar has been ordered for the Mu Pyramid . . . a sacrificial altar."

Cugal became aware that Narlo was staring at his clothes. "It is no longer safe to walk the streets as a First Caste priest, Narlo. You must accept what is."

"I accept that unless we act immediately, it will be too late to save anything we stand for."

"It was too late when Xcane died, my friend," Cugal said.

"I can't accept that. We should have acted before the seven chose a new Lord. We might have been able to pressure them to choose a more moderate path," Narlo said, slamming his fist down on the table. He trembled as the pain flared up through his arm.

"I agree that sometimes we are too accepting for our own good, but in this situation I doubt that we could have altered destiny. Are we not experiencing what our soul records demand of us?" Cugal said.

"Wisdom can erase the records," Narlo snapped. "We haven't been wise."

"What do you suggest?" Nlers asked.

"Force the Xocoman council to make a stand, and then issue a public statement condemning the idea of an army and the Jaguar cult. If enough people supported us, it could force Khatic to change direction."

"What about the more likely result?" Nlers asked. "As soon as it sniffed a rebellion, the army would kill the First and Second Caste priests and the people who supported them."

"Nlers is right, Narlo. Khatic won't step down because some of the people turn against him. The longer the drought continues, the more strongly they will support him. At least half of them probably support him right now."

"That's still a hundred thousand people that are loyal to Talote," Narlo said. "And what are the alternatives?"

"The priests could leave Xocoma," Cugal replied. "But to do that would be to desert our people. None of us would do it."

"The priests could leave and invite their followers to come with them," Nlers proposed.

"To where? To what? To another bloody city that believes like Khatic and Zadic do? To the north, where no one lives because no one can survive?" Cugal demanded. "Even if Khatic were to let them go, people wouldn't abandon the security of their homes for the uncertain and the unknown."

"What would Khatic like us to do?" Narlo asked.

"To disband the Atlantean Circle and peacefully transfer the power of the Xocoman council to Zadic, who would rapidly elevate the Jaguar religion to official status. Shortly thereafter it would probably be reported that we had died in our sleep," Cugal said.

"Or that we'd volunteered our souls for the sacrificial altar," Narlo suggested. "So finally it is a question of leave or die? Desert our people or die?"

Cugal and Nlers were silent.

"Well, then, let's be certain our deaths are not wasted," Narlo said.

"For a while Cugal and I and our servant boys will be living in this cave," Narlo told the fifteen of the Atlantean Circle. "First, I suggest that we try to force the Xocoman council to take a public stand. I think it can be done. But as part of the public statement, we will ask our followers not to rebel openly against the Jaguar. We'll call upon the populace to come to the Mu Pyramid on the Lord's Day, at the best possible astrological time."

"Best time for what?" someone asked.

"We'll seek the advice of a trusted temple astrologer," Nlers said, "to give the event the power to influence generations to come."

Narlo explained his plan in detail and each member voted to accept it. "Each of you is to talk to four members of the council and get them to pledge their support. I don't want a lengthy discussion before the vote because it might create fear. Make sure no one talks to Zita. He's Cakkers's spy. Cugal and I will talk to Xrote the Elder."

"How will you pass through the city?" Xpico the white-skinned Wise One asked.

"I doubt that anyone will recognize us with our hair down, wearing street clothes and bargemen's hats," Cugal said. "But we'll apply some paint just to be sure."

"Alita, as representative of the artisans, can you get some volunteers to paint our message on the city walls the night before we call the general meeting?" Narlo asked. "It will be a short message asking all followers of Talote to attend. The compound priests will also be instructed to announce it at services the night before."

Alita nodded in agreement. The red stripe down her face looked almost black in the torchlight.

"Why can't we give people more time to spread the word and make plans to attend? Many will come from the outlands," someone said.

"Because it would give Khatic time to figure out how to thwart us by keeping them away. By the time Khatic is aware of our plans, all he'll be able to do is gather his own army," Narlo said.

"But the army could prevent us from reaching the Mu Pyramid."

"Fifty-one First Caste priests using crystal rods could hold off an army for a while," someone said.

"But only for a while," Cugal muttered under his breath.

When the meeting was adjourned, Narlo and Cugal left the cave through the priests' basement apartment. Narlo could almost walk normally again, and he breathed deeply without pain, savoring the fragrance of flowering blossoms. The night was warm, the streets nearly deserted. In the distance dogs barked as they always did at night.

"I'd like to check on something," Cugal said.

"I'm just along to get my body working again," Narlo replied, pleased at the thought of a walk for no particular purpose.

The two men avoided the Lord's Way and approached the Mu Pyramid from the back, circling it until they were standing behind a prayer platform in Mu Plaza. From there they could see a door set in the base of the pyramid.

"The clover-leaf entrance? Why, Cugal?"

"I think the Jaguar's attempting to channel the dark powers."

Beneath the great pyramid, leading off from the

entrance they were watching, was a tunnel that connected with four rooms arranged in the shape of a four-leaf clover. Narlo had visited it once when he was first accepted into the priesthood, and had been almost overcome by the intensity of the evil vibrations. There was no record of who originally used the rooms, or for what purpose. Normally the entrance was sealed, but tonight two soldiers stood guard, one on each side of the small door.

Narlo was glad for the warmth of the night and for his friendship with Cugal as they huddled together, watching for any activity.

"Does this remind you of the time we spied on the Second Elder when we were fifteen?" Cugal asked.

"I was just thinking about our student days."

"We caught him under the trees with two women at once."

Narlo smiled, remembering.

Suddenly the door to the clover-leaf rooms swung open and a streak of light shot out into the blackness. The dark shape of a man appeared, framed in the golden glow, and he was followed by another man. Narlo could see from their uniforms that they were soldiers, and he also saw that they were carrying something.

"A body," Cugal whispered.

Soon several more men left through the same doorway. They all wore jaguar mantles except for Zadic, who was dressed in his priestly robes. Khatic was the last man to step out of the light and into the darkness.

CHAPTER TWENTY-TWO

The two soldiers lifted the body and draped the lifeless arms over their shoulders. Khatic, Zadic, and the others walked away toward the House of the Lord. The soldiers walked toward the river.

Narlo and Cugal followed the soldiers at a discreet distance. On the dark street it would appear that the men were helping a drunken friend home, but there was no one on the street to deceive. At the river Narlo and Cugal hid behind a wall. The light of the crescent moon danced across the ripples as the soldiers weighted the dead man's body with rocks and lifted it, one holding his arms, the other his legs. They swung the limp man back and forth a few times before releasing him. He landed with a flat splash a few feet from the shore and quickly sank beneath the inky surface. Hands on their hips, they watched to see if the body would surface. When it didn't, they walked away upriver.

Narlo felt sick.

"All through the spring people have been disappearing," Cugal said. "Three of my priests have reported losses to me. I checked with others of the fifty-two and they have heard the same thing from their priests."

"If Khatic is drawing a dark circle of power, he needs to drink the sacrificial blood every night from the new moon to the new moon," Narlo said, and spat on the ground.

"But people have been disappearing for almost two moon cycles," Cugal said. "Women. Men. Young and old. There is no pattern in those they choose."

"Let's go to Alita's apartment," Narlo said.

"Why?"

"Let me figure it out as we walk."

Narlo was tired by the twenty-block walk to the artisan's apartment. Alita and her lover, Xrika, were still awake, and invited the men into their colorful apartment. Narlo was surprised that Xrika also wore the red stripe, but on the right side of her face. Narlo and Cugal took turns telling them about what they had seen and heard.

"Here is what I want to write on walls throughout the city . . . tonight," Narlo said.

KHATIC HAS STOLEN SIXTY CITIZENS FOR A
NIGHTLY SACRIFICE TO INCREASE HIS POWER

Alita laughed. "Yes, oh yes!" she said. Xrika also thought it was an excellent idea.

"I'll protect you while you work. Cugal will protect Xrika."

The two women quickly gathered their paints and supplies. Narlo and Alita would work on the north/south streets, Cugal and Xrika on those that ran east/west. Standing with his crystal rod ready and his psychic energy fully charged, Narlo watched Alita quickly paint the bright red glyphs and symbols that spelled out the message. By dawn they had encountered only a few farm workers who had risen early to make their way to the fields, and thirteen walls shouted out their accusations against the Lord of Xocoma.

"I must sign them," Alita said after she had finished the first sign.

"Absolutely not," Narlo replied.

"Yes. If I don't, they'll beat and kill other artisans to find out who painted them. This way, they'll know. Then Xrika and I will go underground with you and Cugal."

Narlo reluctantly agreed, and before sunrise the two men and two women were safely back in the cave.

"They'll paint over the signs as soon as they're reported," Cugal said.

"Yes, but by then thousands will have seen them and they will spread the message to those who missed it," Alita countered.

"I think I'd make a better revolutionary than a priest," Narlo said, staring into the flickering torchlight and tossing his jade-and-crystal rod from one hand to the other.

"Past-life bleed through," Xrika said, and laughed.

"Let's go to sleep," Cugal said, lying down on his pallet.

The two women lay together. Narlo's body ached from the night's exertion and he knew he wouldn't sleep. Sitting cross-legged in the sacred prayer position, his spine straight, his hands on his knees, he stared at the small flame before him and acknowledged the four holy worlds: the physical world of matter and the senses, the astral world of imagination and out-of-body travel, the mental world of intuition and psychic senses, and the spiritual world of Talote and the principles of his faith.

As in heaven, so on earth. As in heaven, so on earth. He visualized a mandala—a cross with the four points representing air, fire, earth, and water. *I open*

the seals. I ask for guidance in my acts of intention.
Narlo held the sacred symbol in his mind for a long
time until the visions surfaced. They faded, then
surfaced again before his inner eyes. He watched,
detached, as images of his beloved city turned
bloodred and a dark cloud slowly settled over the
pyramids and temples, the palaces and the apartments. When there was nothing but blackness, he
shivered and wanted to cry out, but the blackness
began to fade until the city reemerged—except that it
wasn't Xocoma. It was another city, a larger, taller
city. Strange. *A city of the future.* On the walls of many
buildings he could see the sacred symbol. As the
vision faded for the last time, Narlo knew that the
message of the Atlanteans would survive.

The following afternoon, as Narlo and Cugal made
their way through the back streets to the working place
of the Temple Astrologer, they noticed that all the
message walls had been painted over.

The walls of the large room were covered with
charts and maps. In the center of the room was a
polished wooden table. Narlo and Cugal sat on one
side, and Xterit, the Temple Astrologer, sat on the
other. Xterit was thin as a stick, with a hooked nose
and white hair that covered his eyes.

"Eleven days from now, just at midday, on the
Lord's Day. It's the most powerful time this entire
spring," Xterit said.

"Powerful? Will the message last for generations?"
Narlo asked.

"If it's charged with enough energy. That's the
positive side if you choose this time—but there's
another side."

Narlo and Cugal looked at each other and then back
at the astrologer.

"It's a good time for the message, but a bad time for those who deliver it."

"Isn't there another time that would—"

"Not for three years," Xterit said quietly.

"Khatic is in a rage," Xrote the Elder was telling Narlo and Cugal. They had surprised him at his apartment compound just before he was to conduct services. "He suspects that you, Narlo, are responsible for the wall messages. His soldiers have searched the city for you, and I suspect you'll be condemned as an enemy of the nation at tonight's temple services."

"Will he make a public statement about the disappearances?"

"I'm sure he'll say that those people all left the city because the Xocoman council isn't doing enough to pacify the gods. Few will accept it, but what can they do?"

Xrote was a small man in his sixties, with intense eyes and an effeminate manner. He lacked the strength of his predecessor, but he was honest and dedicated to the religious concepts of the Xocoman council. Narlo explained his plan and asked for Xrote's support.

"If you had any idea how enraged Khatic is about the wall messages, you wouldn't ask this."

"He's upset because he's been caught murdering people!" Narlo flung his bargeman's hat on the floor in frustration. "What do you think is going to happen if we don't make a stand?"

Xrote the Elder didn't answer for a while. "It will only further enrage the Lord of Xocoma."

"That isn't an answer to my question," Narlo shot back, pointing his index finger at the face of the Master Speaker.

"Narlo!" Cugal said. "Wait for me out in the patio."

The Master Speaker's patio was larger than most in the city. Eight other members of the Xocoman council who lived here were gathered by the temple at the far end of the enclosure, waiting for their superior to emerge from his apartment and conduct the prayer ritual. They acknowledged the Atlantean but did not invite him to join them. Along the south wall spring flowers swayed in the warm breeze. From behind the temple came the gobbling sound of turkeys.

Obviously they eat well, Narlo thought, disgusted with the other priests. He was disgusted with himself as well. He grasped the crystal rod beneath his toga and realized he wanted to confront the Lord of Xocoma face to face. To the death. *It would make death meaningful.*

Cugal and Xrote emerged from the apartment together. Cugal thanked the Master Speaker. Narlo nodded.

"Will he vote with us?" Narlo asked Cugal, as they made their way down a narrow street to their cave.

"Yes, no thanks to you," Cugal said. "You must control yourself, Narlo. We have to do this our way, not Khatic's way."

"I'm sorry. Deep down inside I know that. But out here," he said, raising a fist in the air as they walked, "I want to stop Khatic the only way he understands."

"You can't appear at the Xocoman council to vote," Cugal said.

"But you can carry my written testimony."

Ten days later Narlo sat on a ledge in the hills overlooking Xocoma. The city glistened white in the late afternoon sun. Below him field workers were gathering in groups to make their way home again. Empty barges dotted the river. Far down a road leading out of the city, Narlo watched a figure moving in his direction.

The sun had touched the horizon by the time Cugal reached him.

"I haven't been up here since we were kids," Cugal said.

"The vote?"

"Yes. Tomorrow at midday we deliver the message to the people. Alita has organized the artists, and tonight they will see that notice of the meeting appears on walls throughout the city. Word has also gone out to the compound priests, and they'll announce it at tonight's services."

Narlo smiled to himself, wondering how many would come.

CHAPTER TWENTY-THREE

Tanzel trembled as he braided his master's hair by the flickering torchlight.

"I want to go with you," the boy said, his voice quivering as he fought to control himself.

"No. And if I don't come back, you are to return to your parents in the merchant community. Because you are my servant, the soldiers might seek you out."

"I don't care what they do to me. I want to be with you."

"I care what they do to you, Tanzel. You must live to spread our message. Now, there's nothing more to discuss."

Narlo was dressed formally for a meeting of the Xocoman council: white tunic, kilt, and sandals; around his neck was the sacred symbol inlaid with jade and obsidian. Tanzel stood where the darkness hid his tears. He clenched his hand until his nails bit into his palm.

"Tanzel, my mantle?"

"Here, master," Tanzel said, looking down to hide his red eyes. He stepped into the light, holding Narlo's red-feathered mantle.

"Tanzel, Tanzel." Narlo took the mantle and set it

down. Putting his arms gently around the boy, he soothed him as if he were a small child. Tanzel's arms locked around Narlo, the tears coursing down his cheeks.

"Tanzel, if enough people support us today, Khatic will be forced to change his direction."

"How many people would that be?" Cugal asked. Narlo glanced up at his friend and saw Alita and Xrika standing next to him, waiting to join the march to the pyramid.

"If half the people of Xocoma attended, it would be a show of force Khatic couldn't ignore," Narlo said.

"A hundred thousand people couldn't fit into the pyramid plaza," Alita pointed out.

"I know, but the fact that they tried would not go unnoticed," Narlo said emphatically.

"Do you think Khatic will try to stop us?" Xrika asked.

Cugal answered. "I think he's run out of patience. He'll move against us, but not before he sees how many attend."

"Let us prepare," Narlo suggested.

The four formed a circle and began to chant: "Ohmmmm nama talaaaaa, ohmmmm nama shelaaaa." The sound filled the cave, echoing through the volcanic tunnels as if thousands were calling down the divine white light. Waves of energy entered the chanters' crown chakras and poured through their energy centers, until the explosive surge of serpent fire ascended to flood their minds and bodies with power and awareness.

The four left the cave through the apartment exit, where they were joined by the six priests in residence. The sun was almost directly above them as the ten walked away from the patio and down the alley to the Street of Balam-Ti. Hundreds of people were making their way toward the Mu Pyramid. Most looked anxious but determined, and a cheer went up as soon as they saw the priests.

The ten crossed the street, each priest carrying a crystal rod poised and ready, and made their way down the alley to the Lord's Way. There were no soldiers in sight. The Lord's Way was so crowded they could barely wend their way through the throng, but as soon as people noticed them, they made way. Some shouted encouragement, and some condemned Khatic for his bloody deeds.

The other members of the Xocoman council were already lining the stairs that reached to the top of the great Mu Pyramid. The base of the pyramid was crowded with Second Caste priests and supporters, including Nlers and Xpico. Narlo, Cugal, and the other six priests from the compound continued their climb, filing past their fellow council members until they reached a step that was unoccupied. Narlo stood two thirds of the way up the pyramid; Cugal was several steps above him. Other priests took up their positions, until the line extended all the way to the top, where Xrote the Elder stood before the flames, his arms extended upward in silent prayer.

Below were thousands of cheering, milling people. *How many? How many? Not enough. Maybe one out of every eight or nine. Not enough!*

Narlo looked past the crowd assembled at the foot of the pyramid and scanned the horizon, from the snowcapped mountains and irrigated fields green with new life to the barren fields waiting for rain. He looked across the rooftops of his beloved city. Thousands of apartments, temples, and workshops gleamed in the midday sun. And he thought about the people in those buildings who were either afraid to attend or just didn't care enough. *You've chosen a future of fear*, he thought sadly.

"Ohmmmmm," intoned the people as the sound ascended from the streets in soothing waves.

The conch trumpets rang out from the four corners. The sound of muted drumming, whistles, and clay flutes caressed Narlo's mind like a lover's touch.

"In the divine name of the Giver of All Life, I open to the light," came Xrote the Elder's words. They were quickly echoed by the priests, the phrases rolling harmoniously down the stairs and then fanning out through the swaying people.

As the opening ritual continued, the people responded with renewed energy and enthusiasm. "We seek the light of the Giver of Life. We seek the light of the Giver of Life," they chanted.

Xrote the Elder addressed them. "People of Xocoma," he said. "For generations, the council has taught the Atlantean path of love and self-responsibility. Those of you gathered here today understand that there is no one to blame for our circumstances. All is a test, but wisdom can change circumstances. We can take positive action to create positive change. When we stop questioning and speaking out against the things we know are wrong, we give permission for our rights to be taken from us.

"Khatic, the Lord of Xocoma, and the Lord's Elders want to destroy your religion so they can replace it with the religion of the Jaguar. Ours is the power of light and love. The Jaguar represents the power of darkness and fear. The battle lines have been drawn. The Xocoman council does not want you to resist with force. Instead, send your antagonists light and love. Resist with the power of awareness. Alert others. Apathy is a betrayal of all you believe in. Apathy can destroy your temples and lay waste to your city.

"No one can control you as long as you accept what

you know to be so. No matter what the outcome of this battle, the oppressor cannot touch our souls. We will return. We can choose to return together, to carry the torch of light as a shared goal. Let it be every seven hundred years."

Twenty-five thousand people began to chant, "Seven hundred years. Seven hundred years." Their voices thundered as one, shattering the silence like the voice of a god descended from the sky to proclaim the future. Their arms raised, their eyes closed, they swayed like waves on a wind-driven sea.

Narlo shivered at his people's response and started to pray silently. In the distance he heard the first screams. Spear-carrying soldiers emerged from behind the temples on the other side of the Lord's Way, half a block north. Terror-stricken, the people scattered in every direction as the armed men advanced into the street. Looking toward the Oag Pyramid, Narlo saw six rows of red-helmeted soldiers running down the Lord's Way toward them.

The sound of war drums announced the attack to those who did not yet perceive the danger. Hysteria exploded into panic, and people tried to run, crushing some against walls and trampling others under foot. Then conch trumpets joined the war drums, and Narlo saw soldiers with raised spears and short swords spring simultaneously from all directions, shutting off all avenues of escape. Now the people began milling around inside these human barriers, uncertain and afraid.

Narlo was contemplating what action to take when the trumpets and drums suddenly stopped. The silence was deafening. The people froze. Sweat ran off Narlo's forehead, stinging his eyes. He wiped his eyes with the sleeve of his tunic and breathed deeply, drawing up his energy as he squeezed the jade-and-crystal rod. Behind him a priest dropped something and he heard it bounce down the steps with a hollow, ringing sound. Below him he watched the soldiers slowly step back, opening escape routes to the thousands who filled the streets and surrounding plazas. The crowd hesitated momentarily. Then, as if shot from a sling, they surged down the streets and alleys, quickly emptying the area. Narlo guessed that at least fifty bodies lay crushed beneath their feet and that there were several thousand armed soldiers standing ready to move in for the kill. As the last of the throng disappeared, the soldiers closed ranks, surrounding the Xocoman council of priests and those of their supporters who were still gathered at the pyramid.

"Traitors!" The word rang out, filling the plaza with the sound of hate. Narlo watched Khatic, dressed as the jaguar, march into the plaza, followed by dozens of archers who fanned out on either side of him. "Will your crystal rods stop obsidian arrows?" he asked with a cruel laugh. The archers drew their bows. At a single beat of the war drum, they let the arrows fly. Priests a quarter of the way up the pyramid fell, some rolling down the stairs, some sliding down the steep sides of the pyramid.

Narlo felt Cugal's arm on his shoulder and looked at him. Cugal didn't say a word, but the despair in his eyes said it all. Narlo nodded helplessly.

"Drop your weapons, priests, or your supporters will be the next to die." The archers reloaded and drew their bows. Khatic pointed at the base of the pyramid, said something to his men, and several soldiers ran quickly up the stairs and grabbed Nlers, Xpico, and two other Wise Ones. The four were escorted to Khatic, who bellowed, "I release you to return to the stars. Pheladians are no longer welcome in Xocoma."

The soldiers marched the Wise Ones away. Narlo raised his rod high above his head and threw it down, shattering the jade and crystal. Soldiers armed with spears rushed up the stairs, motioning the priests to descend. By the time Narlo reached the Lord's Way, he didn't see Khatic. An officer dressed as a jaguar instructed his prisoners to follow the soldiers, and the group was surrounded by a rectangle of armed men, spears ready. Narlo estimated that there were thirty-five First Caste priests and at least two hundred supporters, most of them Second Caste priests. With the exception of the Wise Ones, all the members of the Atlantean Circle had been captured.

They marched south on the Lord's Way, across the river, past the walls of Palace Square and deserted Market Square. Finally, outside of the city, they came to a newly-dug pit the depth of three grown men. The prisoners were sent shuffling single file down the steep ramp into the gaping mouth of death. When the last of their number was at the bottom, workers dug away the ramp, tossing each shovel of dirt over the heads of the prisoners.

Narlo brushed the dirt from his hair and scowled up at the diggers and soldiers who looked down on him from above.

"Khatic didn't have this dug overnight," Cugal said.

"I thought they'd kill us on the sacrificial altar," a voice said.

"The gods aren't interested in traitors," another voice answered.

"Are they going to bury us now?"

Dread spread among the group. There was enough room for twice their number standing up, but Narlo doubted they could all lie down at one time. Xrote the Elder quickly moved to calm them, and assigned several men to dig a latrine with their hands in one corner of the pit.

At sunset only four soldiers were visible from

below, one at each corner. A few priests started chanting a mantra, and everyone joined them, drawing the harmonies of peace and love from deep within. "Ohmmm nama Taalootee. Ohmmm nama Taalootee." Narlo watched the crimson sky turn cobalt blue and smiled. He had met his destiny, and he accepted it.

CHAPTER TWENTY-FOUR

"Atlantean," bellowed Khatic.

Narlo looked up to see the Lord of Xocoma standing at the edge of the pit, illuminated by the first rays of the sun. His hands were on his hips. He was dressed as an officer, and wore the mantle of the jaguar. A rattlesnake loincloth was wrapped about his hips.

"Up here, Atlantean."

Soldiers tossed a rope into the pit. At the end was a knot the size of two hands.

Narlo made his way through his friends to the rope. He wrapped it around one leg, then placed both feet on the knot and grasped the rope with his hands. The soldiers quickly hoisted him up as his body banged against the dirt wall, scraping his arms and legs. Two soldiers pulled him over the edge, and he stood facing Khatic.

Derisive laughter greeted the Atlantean as the two men faced each other at arm's length. "Seven hundred years?" Khatic cleared his throat and spat on him. Now the soldiers laughed too.

"If you're coming back in seven hundred years, I'll swear on my father's grave I'll be there as well." He spat out the words contemptuously and laughed again, a long, insane laugh that nearly stopped the hearts of those in the pit.

"If you believed in rebirth, you'd be living a different life today," Narlo said calmly. He looked directly into Khatic's black eyes, ablaze with fury, and smiled serenely.

"You smile now, Atlantean. Do you think you'll be smiling when I bury you?" Khatic roared.

Narlo didn't respond.

"Answer me!" Khatic's anger turned to scalding fury.

Narlo's smile broadened as confidence deepened his serenity.

"Stupid fool," Khatic bellowed. He struck Narlo in the chest, knocking him back into the pit. Those below scrambled out of the way as the Atlantean landed and lay in the dirt, his body twisted terribly.

"Narlo." Cugal was immediately beside him, tears streaming down his face. He saw that his friend's back was broken.

"What does it matter?" Narlo gasped, trying to smile as he looked up into his friend's eyes.

"Oh, Narlo, leave your body and do not return," Cugal begged.

"There's no pain. No feeling. Later."

"You know how to leave. Please."

"I'll see this through, my Cugal."

Cugal sat with Narlo's head in his lap, gently stroking his forehead. There was no water and no food. At midday twenty more people were thrown into the pit. Two died. Most were hurt. The survivors told of the terrible discord and civil strife that reigned in Xocoma.

"They're digging more pits," said a man with a broken arm. "It's the end of our world."

"Last night the artisan section was in flames," recalled a woman who had been thrown naked into

215

the pit. Someone had given her a dirty tunic to wrap around herself, and there was dried blood on her legs. "Seven men raped me," she said as tears left furrows in the dirt on her face.

That night the sky glowed orange in the direction of Xocoma. Xrote the Elder led the chanting of the sacred mantras, accompanied by the terrible sound of distant war drums.

By the following midday a hundred more people had been thrown into the pit. In the afternoon Narlo gasped, and Cugal placed his ear to Narlo's lips to hear his fading words.

"I love you, my friend. I'll always love you," he said, and died.

At sunset soldiers suddenly surrounded the pit and began to shovel dirt over the heads of the prisoners. No one cried. No one screamed. No one resisted. The only sounds were the dry swishing of the dirt as it fell and the serene notes of the mantra that drifted up and across to the fearful city, to inspire the dreams of the 25,000.

SECTION

IV

Return Trip

CHAPTER TWENTY-FIVE

"Welcome aboard Delta flight 1742 to Mexico City," said the pretty flight attendant. Tara and I smiled at each other and held hands.

"Excited?" I asked.

She nodded.

The writing of the Teotihuacan/Xocoma story was completed on September 6, 1989. Five days later my wife and I were on our way to the Teotihuacan Archeological Zone. I hadn't been there in fifteen years. Tara had never been there in this life. I wanted to check on some details and view the city through more understanding eyes. Tara was anxious to get a first look at this ancient civilization that had become such a consuming part of her current reality.

When the plane had reached cruising altitude, I opened my briefcase and pulled out two file folders. One was marked THE END, the other AFTER A.D. 581. Each was thick with letters my staff had sorted for me. I'd read them before, but now that the book was finished, I wanted to review again what others had experienced.

Barbara May, Tucson: My favorite astrologer wrote

me a letter in January 1988 to tell me about a conversation she had had many years earlier with Wassily Kandinsky, channeled through David Paladin. David had died in December 1985, and as I looked out the window of the plane, I thought about David and Kandinsky and the days in Groom Creek, Arizona, when the Teotihuacan story first began to unfold.

Barbara wrote: "According to Kandi, David and I were buried alive in Teotihuacan. We were buried because of what we believed and what we knew. They had to get rid of us and obliterate any trace of our ever having lived at all. Kandi said 'several hundred' of us died this way and it was pretty gruesome."

Mary Ellen Mizuta, Shoreline Hypnosis Clinic, Seattle: "I must reply to your Teotihuacan research project. For as long as I can remember I have been terrified of being buried alive. Now I know why.

"Question: If the 25,000 agreed to come back every seven hundred years to pass on knowledge, who's to say the murderers do not come back every seven hundred years to block this process? Fear and control is the motto of most Fundamentalists, even though they don't recognize it. These people scare me, as does anyone who tries to force a religion down one's throat or thinks their way is the only way. People should be free to choose their own beliefs without being crucified for them. We're acting out the same scenario over again, only with new bodies and new scripts. Let's pray that the outcome is better this time."

Faith Wallace, Barrington, New Hampshire: Faith told of a meditation group she belongs to and how, after hearing of my interest in Teotihuacan, she decided to focus on the ancient city.

"One person visualized a leader, a tall, well-built man standing above a crowd. She described his attire and particularly remembered the green stone ornament over his heart (I assume this was a pendant). He also held a crystal rod.

"Another member of the group experienced a group burial and insisted that it was not a sacrifice. She heard beautiful music as those souls died and ascended to the spirit world."

Dr. Tom Holloway, Carmichael, California: "In the Teotihuacan regression you conducted in Palm Springs, I experienced being captured and bound. Soldiers were questioning me about the location of those who had gone into hiding. To extract the answers, they had used a mallet and chisel-like object to break the bones under my right and left eyes, leaving the eyeballs protruding from the sockets. They used the same process to break both clavicles [collar bones]. I was not afraid to die, and did not reveal the location of those who were in the underground tunnels."

Mary Ellen Pignatelli, Belleville, New Jersey: "When I read the first article on Teotihuacan in your magazine, I was at work. Things were slow, and my mind began to drift in and out of alpha. I started to get a message, as if my mind were picking up a CB radio. I started to do automatic writing, and the result was a 'message' from one of the seven. I don't know if I was one of the seven or if the message was coming through me, but here it is:

"'I am one of the seven. We did not do it for revenge, but because our own thinking had seduced us into finding a way to destroy you. We were sent there to be tested, and the seven failed the test. But the sixteen also failed the test that was given them. They did not find a way to overcome the thinking of the seven. We have also reincarnated every seven hundred years, because the strength of your souls have called us to be with you. And we have given you challenges. I have not come here now to challenge you, because over the centuries you have learned to incorporate the thinking of the seven into your own thinking, and it is that thinking and not us that you have to overcome. I have suffered centuries of guilt, not for killing the several hundred, but because I knew what you knew. We had the knowledge to create our world. (I did not function as an *I*, but rather as part of a whole—the *seven* were one who fell prey to the thinking of their leader.)

"'There is no reason to apologize for killing the priests. I still have my pride. As one of the seven I was controlled because I forgot that I could not be controlled. You must let go now. The priests who vowed to come back every seven hundred years made a mistake in thinking that there was some special importance in retrieving the lost information. The answer is not to reincarnate together. It is to let go. You must let go of the life you lived in Mexico. I am just learning to separate myself from the seven. I didn't let go before because I thought it was too important. Let's be happy together. I forgive you. I forgive myself. Be big-hearted—let the seven go. By remembering the devastation, you are opening yourself to the leader's thinking again, and it will live again. Turn to the light. Remember what you knew, what we all knew before the devastation and the mistake.'"

Anita Marie Aiston, Clay, New York: "The regression took me back to a time well after the reign of the seven. I experienced this in spirit not in the physical body. All I can relate is an overpowering feeling of sadness at what I saw. The temples were deserted and partially in ruins. The people ignored them, but the children continued to play in them. The people had lost the ability to 'look up' from their everyday life and remember the grandeur of the old civilization. It was obvious to me that the magic and spirit of the people was gone."

Pat Steiner, Las Vegas: "In your Sedona Psychic Seminar, at the Saturday-night session conducted by Don Tinling, I had a traumatic regression experience. Following the time of upheaval, I saw myself in a large room where I taught children how to read the mystery books. I had a crystal stuck like a magnet on my forehead. I taught reading by placing the crystal on each page of the book. I also taught my students to read the usual way so the unbelievers wouldn't know how we usually did it. When I was discovered, the soldiers cut out my tongue so I could no longer teach the old ways."

Sydney Taylor, Columbia, California: "In A.D. 650 people from the north are taking over and it is a time of famine. There are too many people and the food sources are running out. There is not enough rain for the crops and too much luxury and overindulgence by the rich. The practice of human sacrifice and cannibalism repulses me, and I belong to a group of activists from the gentle time."

Sandy Bruce, Syracuse: "A.D. 712—The ruler has no psychic ability. He believes the ability is a weakness—'soft.' He says we have to have a strong government and large army. White death is coming in like a plague. Something from the volcano. The land turns white. Vegetation dies. First the goats and children die, then the meat eaters—the soldiers. People scatter in every direction."

I put the file folders back in my briefcase when the flight attendants began to serve lunch.

"What do you know historically about the collapse of Teotihuacan?" Tara asked.

"By the 600s Teotihuacan the city was declining and its enormous influence throughout Mesoamerica began to disappear. Sometime in the 700s it suffered a major disaster. Sculpted columns were torn apart and thrown into a pit. The stairway of the Oag [Moon] Pyramid was purposely wrecked, and the plaza structures and platforms were destroyed. Anything wooden was burned."

"You sound like an encylopedia," Tara said, and laughed.

"I feel like one after spending months on this project. There's plenty of archeological evidence to show that by around A.D. 650 many of the people who still lived in the city were the victims of armed assault. The fact that the ceremonial centers were ravaged suggests that an outside invasion may have taken place. Yet the destruction was so methodical that some scientists suspect the priests destroyed their own temples.

"Here, let me read you something in *The Ancient Kingdoms of Mexico* by Nigel Davies." I took the book out of my briefcase and found the last paragraph of the chapter on the "Decline and Fall of Teotihuacan":

"Modern study and ancient metaphor stress the impact of a collapse, whose shock waves were felt throughout ancient Mexico. Power crumbled and the economy faced ruin as the main arteries of commerce were severed. The demand for luxury goods, confected for Teotihuacan's nobles, plummeted, and the wealth derived from this trade vanished overnight. Such convulsions were followed by a spiritual crisis that had its material effects; when the city lost its religious aura, it was visited by no more of those pilgrims, who, like the modern tourist, added much to the trade balance. The fall of Teotihuacan, like that of Rome three centuries before, left in its wake a disordered world, whose surviving cities were like planets in orbit round an extinct sun."

"I think he has it backward," Tara said. "I'll bet the spiritual crisis and a hostile army caused the other cities in Mesoamerica to stop trading with Teotihuacan."

"I agree," I said.

The cabin loudspeaker clicked on. "We are now preparing for our descent into Mexico City," the flight attendant said.

CHAPTER TWENTY-SIX

"From the moment the plane touched down, until we arrived here at the Archeological Zone, my heart's been beating double time," Tara said.

"The cab ride didn't help."

Our driver believed in one speed—as fast as the cab would go. In heavy traffic on a two-lane highway he had passed a bus, forcing an oncoming driver off the road to avoid a head-on collision. At that point Tara tapped him on the shoulder and said, in Spanish, "Enough. We have three young children at home." At dusk we arrived safely at the Hotel Villas Arqueologicas Teotihuacan.

Tuesday, September 12, 1989: It was a warm summer morning, and we enjoyed our half-mile walk from the hotel to the Archaeological Zone. Admission was 1200 pesos (forty-five cents). Holding hands, we walked out onto the deserted Street of the Dead (Lord's Way). It was 8:05 A.M.

After nearly eight years together, my wife and I still feel like honeymooners. Today we were awestruck kids, running up and down the steps of the pyramids, then from one end of the mile-long street to the other and back again. We took hundreds of pictures and checked a lot of points in the book for accuracy.

We stopped twice to catch our breath on the steep steps of the Sun Pyramid (Mu Pyramid). From its top I could easily imagine standing before a blazing fire, looking down the steps at the white-robed priests arrayed like sentinels and the thousands of citizens gathered in the huge plaza to testify to their faith.

The only negativity Tara felt all day was in response to what I'd called the "landing platform" in the thirty-six-acre Citadel (Palace Square). She felt that it was used at one time for public torture and/or sacrifice.

"Well, Narlo, what are your feelings about being here?" Tara asked over lunch. We sat by a window in the restaurant at the National Museum, looking out over the Citadel three floors below.

"Entirely positive, Cugal." I couldn't help smiling. The fact that my beautiful wife was once my male friend seemed even more plausible now that we were here. "Maybe getting the books together has been an exorcism for me."

"We'll see if there are any visions tonight," she said.

In our past-life regressions, both Tara and I had seen the city as gleaming white, with an abundance of painted decorations and murals. Yet as we explored the ruins, we saw constant evidence that most of the structures were painted red.

"If our psychic information is correct, Khatic continued to have the city painted red after we were gone," Tara said.

"How about doing some automatic writing tonight?" I asked. Tara agreed.

By mid-afternoon a dog had adopted Tara, following us everywhere. "My temple dog," she called it. My wife is a Sagittarius (five planets in Sag), and true to her nature, befriends every animal she sees.

There wasn't enough time to study and photograph everything we wanted to see before the five P.M. closing time, but we would have had to leave anyway because it started to rain as we hobbled back to our hotel. Although we play tennis constantly, we were not used to climbing thousands of stairs, and our legs were very sore. We took a long, hot shower together, made love, and speculated about the feelings of Narlo and Cugal for each other 1400 years earlier.

The only downside to visiting the pyramids is having to fight off the hundreds of hustlers trying to hawk mass-produced souvenirs, including obsidian statues, flutes, copies of Michelangelo's David, and ivory elephants with red eyes. When you tell them no, they simply follow you and keep on talking. When you tell them no in no uncertain terms, they call you an "ugly American."

Although the Club Med hotel is a first class hostelry, when we walked back into our room after dinner, a burglar went out the window. We evidently caught him unawares and he didn't have time to take anything. I always travel with security equipment, including a door-locking system even hotel security can't defeat, but I hadn't felt the need to use it this time. Wrong.

Once the room was secured and we'd called the kids back home in California, I settled down to write and Tara went into trance to do some automatic writing. After the session she explained, "When I got to my temple room, my guide and Phillipoetes [a Greek teacher who helps her paint] were there. They introduced me to a 'light being.' His form was human, but he glowed and I couldn't make out any features."

The Automatic Writing
You are where we were many, many years ago. I

want to say hello and express to you what an honor it is to see you again. I am an alien to your planet and what you know. I'm gathering strength by writing through you. I was there with you, and Narlo, and Nlers, and the others. Your nicknames for each other are what Richard is presenting in the book. I was one of the Atlantean Circle and come in now and again to sway your minds. Xocoma was a most beautiful place. Made of shellacked white paste paint, it gleamed, almost blindingly, in the sunlight. It was not red until the Jaguar people took power.

You do not need to worry about your safety here. You will not be harmed other than with mild indigestion. This is the place that we have hoped Richard will continue to work. What better support than for his best friend in that life to be with him again in this one? You both lived in a palace near the Moon Pyramid. I and others have given Richard the names for the book. Of course the people who live there now have no idea what they speak of. Spanish was not close to our way. Atlantis, the great culture, was the influence and the source of the beautiful names.

I enjoyed being on that sojourn. I came from X219APOLICANO4928. This is the best name I can give you. It is a small developed planet beyond your wildest dreams. But we are all of the same source. Some of you may venture to a different way. Earth people get stuck with gravity thinking just as they want to immediately reincarnate into anything or anywhere. It should be a careful choice. Remember that.

I want to help you with some of the facts that you seek. All the people came almost every day to buy market food. Only priests and certain classes of people were allowed to live in the confines of the temple area. There was no negativity allowed. They considered the lower classes barbaric. Unless attending the rituals or festivals, very few women were allowed in the temple area. Men of other classes were allowed only if they were cleansed and presentable to the gods and priests. They served as laborers who fed the priests and cleaned the palaces, temples, and streets.

(Note: The writing went on to verify many items of information already communicated in the story of Narlo and Cugal, and offered personal advice relating to our metaphysical communications.)

In response to the last questions you're thinking about: You were on the Sun Pyramid when the sword-bearing soldiers took you away and buried you behind the Citadel. You might want to see that. I will be going along with you for the next few days, helping guide you and just being there, because it is so very much fun.

We used Xocoma as a guide for our spacecraft, but we landed over where the highway is now. We needed much room to land. Any other questions, please call on me.

Phillipoetes will help you to do automatic drawing if you want to later. Have a good trip, and there will be no further problems with thieves. You caught on to that one. The management, of course, played coy, but they know this happens very often. The thieves have keys to get into the rooms. The window they cannot get into.

I am most glad to be able to share with you on your great journey. A time and place that was dear to all of us. Be well and "Xopalato"—it means 'peace be with you always' in Atlantean. Your future friend from your past.

XK8

XO

(He drew a little arrow to the XO and wrote "Atlantis.")

The handwriting now changed completely and Tara's spirit guide finished the communication with two pages of personal information. That night we both dreamed of Xocoma as it once was.

Wednesday, September 13, 1989: Tara and I took off on foot through the village of San Juan, a rural area of ramshackle homes and plowed fields dotted with the ruins of apartments and palaces I hadn't seen in 1974.

Tetitla is an example of a huge apartment compound that housed hundreds of people. Many of the remaining walls are covered with fragments of murals. There was a communal bath, an outdoor patio, and a temple. The compounds date from between A.D. 300 and A.D. 600.

Atetelco was home to many priests and much like the apartment of Narlo and Cugal as I had seen it in past-life regression. Tara made friends with the caretaker, who spent over an hour showing us around and explaining everything he knew about the site. The restored sections are exquisite. An altar sits in the center of the main patio. Some of the rooms had fire pits. Rainwater falling on the apartment roofs was channeled into a decorative waterfall that flowed into a cistern. Throughout Teotihuacan there is evidence of water systems that were used to supply the baths, sewers, and reflective pools.

In the "White Patio" are three reconstructed buildings. We cringed at the original red mural that pictures a jaguar holding a heart in its paw. The caretaker ended his tour by showing us a human jawbone, and pointed out where sophisticated dental work had been performed on two of the teeth using a drill and other tools.

We found the ruins of two large stone apartment

compounds in the middle of corn and bean fields. As we started across one field, I noticed a pottery shard —"thin orange"—the pottery Teotihuacan was famous for manufacturing. I was elated. Tara was also picking up pieces. As we took a few more steps into the field we realized that there were literally millions of shards, not only thin orange, but all kinds of pottery, many with painted designs. Flakes of obsidian were everywhere. Tara found an obsidian razor—perfectly cut and angled—the product responsible for much of the city's wealth and power.

Our interest in the field attracted some young children, who offered to sell us a broken bowl, a toy doll, and fragments of sculpture—clearly originals found in these fields.

The people living around the ruins have often added to an ancient wall to make a home, or used the original stones to build a new structure. I took a picture of a Teotihuacan design carved into an ancient block of stone that is now part of the back wall of a shack.

As far as we walked, we found the remains of buildings and stone walls. Cows and sheep were grazing on what had once been a bustling city, and corn was growing where walled apartments had once stood.

We ate a late lunch in a tent that served as a roadside restaurant. It was run by two women; one waited on customers while the other hand-pressed tortillas, cooking them on an oil drum converted into a wood-burning stove. The other six customers were local Mexicans. We had chicken tacos, rice, cheese tortillas, and Carta Blanca beer. A gourmet feast.

"It's taken me until now to feel at home in Mexico again," I said at lunch.

"I've been perfectly at ease all day," Tara told me.

"You just needed to get out with the common people again."

We hiked back to the Archeological Zone about three P.M., trying for the second day to photograph the Moon Pyramid (Oag Pyramid) in the afternoon sunshine.

"The clouds beat us again," I said, emerging from the Palace of the Jaguars just in time to see the sun disappear. We climbed to the top of the pyramid, hoping it would clear up, but instead the great grandfather of all thunderstorms manifested itself within minutes.

"How long will it last?" Tara asked a girl in the bookstore at the edge of the zone.

"One or two hours," she said.

So we begged two plastic book bags to use as rain hats and set off on the two-mile hike back to the hotel, laughing every time we looked at each other.

Before going to sleep that night, Tara went into trance and did some automatic drawing. The first page looks like two pieces of sculpture separated by a pond or reflective pool. Below the drawing is a line of strange-looking symbols followed by some words of explanation: "This is in the pyramid that is called the Moon. Excavate needed to find this. It is dark now."

The second page was a drawing of a jaguar with the same symbol writing beneath it, and the third page was just symbols. The fourth page had a note at the top in Tara's handwriting: "Phillipoetes led me into a temple to talk to this man."

The rest of the page is handwriting unlike Tara's, which says, "I am not an artisan, but this is what a few of the murals looked like, and, of course, our writing. The fish pond can be found in the Pyramid Moon. I was young when the priests were sent to death, but they were remembered by many." The signature appears first in the strange writing, then beneath it is the name "Xypotic."

Thursday, September 14, 1989: In telling the story of Narlo and Cugal, I had envisioned the Palace of the Wise Ones to be just a little south of the Sun Pyramid on the east side of the street. When I actually explored the ruins, I was surprised to find that this is the site of a unique palace. It is the only building in Teotihuacan where thick layers of mica were used as part of the stone floor. No one has yet figured out why. Another unique feature is an elaborate basement system of tunnels and rooms.

Tara and I skipped breakfast to be at the Archeological Zone when it opened. We seemed to be alone in Teotihuacan for the first two hours, exploring the ruins of the mica floor and the Palace of the Lord where Xcane and Khatic lived. The palace was located a bit off the street; after the heavy rain the day before, we were surprised to find a lot of thin orange pottery shards on the ground around the thick stone walls.

Later, sitting on the top of the Moon Pyramid with Tara's temple dog lounging contentedly between us, we looked out across the city and down the Street of the Dead that stretched out a mile before us. On each side of the street were the ruins of palaces, temples, and apartment compounds.

"The whole civilization revolved around religion, didn't it?" Tara said.

"Maybe it's the reason we're both so averse to organized religion and ritual," I replied. A few tourists were now walking along the Street of the Dead. The sound of the souvenir sellers playing their flutes floated up to us as we sat high above the city.

"Without belief there wouldn't have been a Teotihuacan or a Xocoma," Tara said.

"Sick, huh? A belief is always something you don't

know. You may think you know. You may even be willing to stake your life on the fact that you know, but you don't really know. And belief can always be used against you."

I thought about a book reviewer who said, "If I were a dictator, I'd sure like my subjects to adopt Shirley MacLaine's ideas."

The dictator says, "There's no one to blame for these circumstances but yourself. Obviously, it's your karma to experience this."

"How would you respond to the idea that your acceptance of karma could be used against you?" Tara asked.

"I'd agree it was my karma. But wisdom erases karma, and the wise thing to do would be to over-throw the dictator."

"You're still a militant priest."

At three P.M. we checked into the Hotel Presidente Chapultepec in Mexico City. By three-thirty we were exploring the National Museum of Archeology, en-grossed in the incredible Teotihuacan exhibits. Tara found a sculpture that matched the design she had received in the automatic drawing. It was a unique piece neither of us had seen in any book.

Back in our hotel room, high up on the twenty-third floor, we ordered a late room-service dinner and took turns rubbing each other's aching feet and legs with a soothing balm.

"If you're up to any automatic writing, I've got some questions that relate to what we saw today," I said.

"I can't lie down after that meal anyway," Tara replied.

She settled herself on the bed, propped a pillow up against the headboard, leaned back and went into trance. She'd been writing about twenty minutes when she said, "XK8 wants you to hear what the language

sounded like," Tara said. "Xypotic will speak it for
you."

"Huh?"

"Right now I'm receiving writing from XK8, but he
said, 'You'd better tell Richard. If he hears you
starting to talk in another language, he's going to be
perturbed.'"

"Ol' XK was right!"

"Well, I'm not going to verbally channel. I'll just go
back into my temple room and repeat what he says.
Okay?"

"Okay," I said, sitting at the foot of the bed with
what I'm sure was a very strange look on my face.

Tara quickly went into trance and began to speak. I
won't attempt to translate the words to paper, but
they were unlike anything I'd ever heard. She said,
"They mean, 'I wish you much success with the
book.'"

The Automatic Writing

XK8 sends greetings. I am glad you chose me to
come and speak to you again. I want to help answer
your questions. Your friend Xypotic is here also and
wants to help explain what he wrote to you and speak
to Richard in the Xocoman native tongue. He has not
returned to the earth plane yet because the Jaguars
were such a bloodthirsty people that he didn't want to
come and face those earth people again. Maybe you
could counsel him since you were once one of his
kind. He doesn't trust me since I'm of light and he
isn't sure he wants to be like me either.

Yes, the Wise Ones lived in the palace of mica
floors. There were many underground tunnels. The
people always had something to fear, and they really
did try to use their heads to deal with the situation.
The mica, which was called 'polatia,' is the prettiest
material they had to work with. Plus, it shone like the

stars. Often the ground trembled and they were afraid of the volcano. They reinforced their floors with mica to help protect them from the elements.

This civilization will never see the likes of our spacecraft because you do not have the right gases on earth. It won't be until a future incarnation that you and Richard see space travel. As I have said before, we used the pyramids as a guide. We helped the people with architecture, but they did the work. Laser technology came from Atlantis, and they used some of this. The devices are buried beneath the Sun Pyramid in a secret chamber about four levels down from what is now the ground. It was hidden shortly after the Jaguar people came to haunt Xocoma. They knew by hiding the devices beneath the pyramid they would be found in the far future.

As for your question about the Wise Ones, we left Xocoma and went north. As we had taken earthly bodies, we could not risk living in a destructive society.

The death wheel you observed in the museum was not there until after your time. Neither were a lot of the murals. The colored glaze was easily re-covered in white and repainted to represent jaguar symbols. Some are original.

The Moon Pyramid was closed up at the time of the Jaguar's leaving. They forced many beams to fall, caving in a lot of the inside. The entrance was on the right side when facing the pyramid. The natives didn't realize when refacing it that there was a doorway. The same is true of the Sun Pyramid. Close to the side steps were two doors. Second Caste priests prayed all day, then came out the side doors and went up those stairs. They were not yet holy enough to enter from the front stairs. In the pyramid was a secret teaching place—a school for the very holy and privileged.

Your friend from Xocoma wants to talk to you now.

You should warn Richard that you will speak like this so he isn't perturbed. Go to your temple door and call out.

Saturday, September 16, 1989: Back home in Malibu on an overcast afternoon, we took a long walk on the beach with the young children. Hunter collected pieces of shells. When we stopped to rest, Cheyenne explored the tactile potentials of sand; eating it, throwing it, and trying to get it off her fingers.

"Were we really in another world a few hours ago?" I wondered.

We watched a group of pilot whales swimming through the surf thirty yards from shore. Sandpipers darted in and out of the lapping waves. The gulls stood around us, looking expectantly out to sea.

"What are the most important lessons to be learned from all this exploration?" Tara asked.

"There are so many," I replied, observing my three-year-old son's excitement at finding a shell. "Most important, love doesn't die; it cannot die. It is not limited to the physical boundaries of time and space. To me, we're living examples of that truth.

"But there's another lesson that's important to point out in case anyone misses it. We're living on the earth and we must use worldly methods combined with our spiritual awareness for the greater good. Positive change necessitates positive action. The word 'karma' means 'action.' We have to act. When we stop questioning and speaking out against the things we feel strongly about, we give permission for our rights to be taken away. Indifference and apathy will bury us. People may not be indifferent or apathetic, but ignoring a threat can lead to the same end."

When we got home I looked up a couple of related quotes. Nobel Prize winner Salvatore Quasimodo said, "Indifference and apathy have one name—betrayal." American novelist Stephen Crane said, "Philosophy should always know that indifference is a militant thing. It batters down the walls of cities and murders the women and children amid the flames and the purloining of altar vessels. When it goes away, it leaves smoking ruins, where lie citizens bayoneted through the throat. It is not a children's pastime like mere highway robbery."

Sitting at my desk, I clicked on the computer I hadn't touched for a week. Tara brought me a cup of fresh coffee.

"Going to write the last chapter?" she asked, rubbing the back of my neck.

I nodded.

"I love you," I said. "I'll always love you."

SECTION

V

Scripts to Explore
on Your Own

CHAPTER TWENTY-SEVEN

Receiving Impressions of Past Lives

If you've read this far, you probably wonder if you were part of what happened in Teotihuacan/Xocoma. I believe that many of those drawn to my seminars have attended because they were part of this ancient group. The same is probably true of many who will read this book.

Are you one of the 25,000? While it is fresh in your mind, I'd suggest you ask that question of your own guides and Masters as you go to sleep tonight. Ask that you receive impressions or feelings during the day, and dreams during the night. Also, ask that you remember the dreams literally, not symbolically, immediately upon awakening. And keep a pen and paper by your bed to record your impressions.

Past-life regressions can be directed by a qualified hypnotist, or you may use prerecorded tapes or tapes that you make yourself. You may also induce your own altered state (as you do in meditation), regress yourself and ask your own questions as you perceive impressions.

Anyone can successfully explore their past lives in an altered state of consciousness once they understand how to do it, and if they will *trust* their mental impressions and the images that dance before their inner eye. In my book *Finding Your Answers Within* (Pocket Books, 1989) I explain in detail how to alter your consciousness and make your own self-change and regression tapes. In this book I'll give you a capsulized version of that understanding. If you need additional assistance, refer to *Finding Your Answers Within,* or write me at the address in the back of this book for a catalog of helpful material.

First, entering an altered state of consciousness is *not* a matter of "trancing out." It *is* a matter of relaxing your physical body and focusing your concentration on one thing. Research has proven that when most people watch television, they are in an altered state two thirds of the time.

Next, in past-life regression, the worst thing you can do is try too hard. The idea is to relax and stop thinking. Actually, it is a matter of concentrating without thinking—you want to keep your mind focused on what you are doing and the results you want to achieve without focusing on "how to do it" or wondering "is it happening?" Relax and let impressions emerge from your subconscious mind. Don't try to make it happen. Let it happen.

Next, let go of your expectations about the kind of impressions you'll receive. Some people perceive fantasylike impressions. They see images before their inner eye but feel they're making them up. Others don't "see" a thing. They become aware of an inner knowing, or strong thoughts. I've had people tell me they hear the regression with their inner ear, like imagining a conversation. Occasionally someone will experience dreamlike impressions, but that's the exception, not the rule.

Here's an exercise on how to perceive with your

inner eyes. Right now, with your eyes wide open, imagine yourself walking up to your front door. Now remember everything about the front door of your house or apartment. See everything surrounding the door area. See the doorknob and the keyhole. *[Close the book and take a minute or so to do the exercise.*

That's it. That's how you may perceive past-life impressions in an altered state. Let's try another exercise. This time I want you to close your eyes and just listen to someone called "Babbler" who lives in your head. He's always there and he's always babbling. *So close the book and just listen for a minute or two.*

Did you hear the voice? If not, it was the voice that was saying, "Voice, what voice? I don't hear any voice." Babbler's always there, and you can be assured that he'll provide past-life information if you're not receiving it any other way.

Now that you know how to receive, all that's left is the session itself. To induce an altered state, you can think the induction to yourself, speak it to yourself, or record it. Every hypnotist and meditation leader uses different words, so you can change or paraphrase the words until they are comfortable for you. My company, Valley of the Sun Publishing, markets tapes using many completely different inductions.

The secret to using the induction effectively is to speak in a monotone at a slow pace in an even, uninflected tone of voice, as if you were bored to death, and you'll put everyone to sleep, including yourself. If you experience an altered-state session once a day for two or three weeks, you will attain your natural level and be a "conditioned" subject. Once you've attained this level, you probably won't go deeper with each session. Continuing to work with subjective explorations will, however, result in ever-greater receptivity. In other words, the more you do altered-state regression and psychic work, the better you will get at it.

THE ALTERED STATE TECHNIQUE INDUCTION

First, use deep breathing to relax your body and mind. Take a very deep in-breath, and hold it for as long as you comfortably can. Then let the breath out slowly through slightly parted lips; this allows you to retain the moisture in your mouth. When you think there is no air left in your lungs, contract your stomach muscles and force out any that remains. Then repeat the process. Do this diaphragm breathing for two to five minutes before you begin the regression session. Then, close your eyes, get comfortable and start the tape. When you begin to relax your physical body, play the role, play the part and imagine your body relaxing in response to the suggestions.

BODY RELAXATION SCRIPT

The relaxing power is now entering the toes of both of my feet at the same time. It is moving right on down into my arches . . . into my heels, and up into my ankles. Completely relaxed. Completely relaxed. And the relaxing power now moves on up my legs to my knees, relaxing all the muscles as it goes . . . and now on up my legs to my thighs and to my hips, just completely relaxing. And my full attention is on relaxing my body as the relaxing power now moves on up into the fingers of both of my hands . . . relaxing my hands. And my forearms are relaxing . . . and my upper arms are relaxing. My fingers and hands and forearms and upper arms are now completely relaxed. And the relaxing power moves on down into the base of my spine. Relaxing the base of my spine . . . and beginning to move slowly up my spine . . . up my spine . . . up my spine, and into the back of my neck and shoulder muscles. And the back of my neck and shoulder muscles are now becoming loose and limp . . . loose and limp . . . just completely relaxed. And the relaxing power now moves on up the back of my neck and into my scalp . . . relaxing my scalp. And the feeling of relaxation now drains on down into my facial muscles, relaxing my facial muscles. My jaw is relaxed. I leave a little space between my teeth. And my throat is relaxed. My entire body is now relaxed all over in every way . . . and all tension is gone from my body and mind.

And I now draw a beam of shimmering, iridescent white light down from above. This is the Universal Light of Life Energy . . . the God light. I imagine it . . . I create it with the unlimited power of my mind. And the light enters my crown chakra of spirituality at the top of my head. I feel it beginning to flow through my body and mind . . . flowing through my body and mind, and beginning to concentrate around my heart area. And I now imagine the light emerging from my heart and totally surrounding my body with a protective aura of bright white God light. And I am totally protected. Totally protected. Only my own guides and Masters or highly evolved and loving entities who mean me well will be able to influence me in any way.

(As you begin to deepen the altered state, visualize yourself in a situation in which you are going down, down, down as you count backward from seven to one. This is very important.)

Number seven: deeper, deeper, deeper, down, down, down. Number six: deeper, deeper, deeper, down, down, down. Number five: deeper, deeper, deeper, down, down, down. Number four: deeper, deeper, deeper, down, down, down. Number three: deeper, deeper, deeper, down, down, down. Number two: deeper, deeper, deeper, down, down, down. Number one. And I am now relaxed and at ease and I feel a sense of deepness. I remain consciously aware of my surroundings, but my body is going to sleep . . . to sleep . . . to sleep. Number seven: deeper, deeper, deeper, down, down, down. Number six: deeper, deeper, deeper, down, down, down. Number five: deeper, deeper, deeper, down, down, down. Number four: deeper, deeper, deeper, down, down, down. Number three: deeper, deeper, deeper, down, down, down. Number two: deeper, deeper, deeper, down, down, down. Number one . . . and I am now in a deep, deep altered state of consciousness.

I am relaxed and at ease and feel in balance and in harmony. If at any time I should become upset and desire to awaken, I will simply count up from one to five and say the words, "Wide awake." I am always in total control.

(At this time insert the main programming script that you desire to experience. Six Teotihuacan/ Xocoma related scripts follow the Awakening. After the scripts I offer altered-state tips that will help you to have a successful regression or programming session.)

AWAKENING

In just a moment I am going to awaken to full beta consciousness, feeling as if I've had a nice, refreshing nap. My head will be clear, and I'll think and act with calm self-assurance, feeling glad to be alive and at peace with myself, the world, and everyone in it. I will awaken remembering absolutely everything that I experienced in this altered state of consciousness. On the count of five I will open my eyes and be wide awake. Number one, coming on up now and I sense an expanding spiritual light within. Number two, coming on up and at peace with all life. Number three, coming on up and I sense internal balance and harmony. Number four, I now recall the situation and the room. Number five, wide awake, wide awake!

Script One

Teotihuacan/Xocoma General Past-Life Regression

(Induction first)

In the memory banks of my subconscious mind is a memory of everything that has ever happened to me in this life I am now living, or in any of my past lives. Every thought, every spoken word, every action from every lifetime I have ever lived is recorded in these memory banks. And I am now going to draw forgotten awarenesses to the surface. In so doing I will better understand what influences, restricts, or motivates me in the present.

And in this session I am going to explore a lifetime in the city now called Teotihuacan and once called Xocoma (Sho-coma), if indeed I incarnated in the time of this great civilization. Xocoma existed for a thousand years in central Mexico. It was created around 200 B.C., reached the height of its power and influence around A.D. 500 to A.D. 600, and was in ruins by A.D. 800.

If I incarnated in Xocoma more than once, I will initially experience the most important incarnation. Each time I experience this regression I will explore a different lifetime, until I am aware of them all.

So to begin, it is time to step into a tunnel to my own past. I now create a vivid mental impression of a tunnel, and as I count backward from five to one, I will imagine myself moving through the tunnel into my own past. On the count of one I will see myself in an important or clarifying situation that took place during the Xocoma lifetime.

All right, I'm stepping into the tunnel . . . letting go and beginning to move back in time. Number five, I'm moving through time. I feel myself letting go of the present and moving back into my mental memories. Moving through the tunnel, and way down at the end I see a light. I'm moving toward the light, and on the count of one I'll be there. On the count of one I'll step out of the end of the tunnel and into the light . . . and I'll perceive myself back in Teotihuacan . . . back in Xocoma. Number four, I'm moving through time, allowing it to happen. I feel it happening. I'm moving back in time and picking up speed. Moving toward the light at the end of the tunnel. Number three, I actually feel the sensation of speed as I rapidly move back in time. Moving closer and closer and closer to the light at the end of the tunnel. Number two, I'm getting very close now. I'm almost there. Allow it to happen. Feel it happening. On the next count I'll feel or sense or see myself in an important or clarifying situation that transpired during this lifetime. Number one, I am now there. Allow the impressions to begin to form.

(1½ to 3 minutes silence for past-life impressions)

All right . . . I will remember everything that I am experiencing, but I'll let go of this now and open to perceive more information about my Xocoman incarnation. First, I'll perceive the year of this lifetime as it relates to the present calendar system. I'll simply trust the numbers as they come into my mind. The first number of the year is ____. Second number ____. Third number ____. And is that B.C. or A.D.?

And now, it is time to perceive more about my involvement in this life. What did I do for a living? My trade, occupation, or the primary way I spent my time? Allow vivid impressions to come in.

(1½ to 3 minutes silence)

All right, let go of this and move on to experience an overall awareness of the society at this time. Perceive vivid impressions of the city and how I interacted with the environment. Allow the impressions to come in now.

(1½ to 3 minutes silence)

All right, I'll continue to remember everything I observe and learn, but it's now time to perceive vivid impressions that relate to my religious beliefs and how I interact with my religion and those who represent the religion. The impressions are forming now.

(1½ to 3 minutes silence)

And now, let go of this, and it's time to perceive information about my personal life in Xocoma: where I live, how I dress, what I eat, and the people who are important to me. The impressions are beginning to come in.

(1½ to 3 minutes silence)

All right, it's time to further explore my city, which is known for its great sculpture and wall paintings. Also, many festivals take place in the city. It's time once again to observe the city during the time of a festival. I'll perceive the costumes, the food, the activities, and the reason for the festival. Everything. The impressions are now beginning to flow into my mind.

(1½ to 3 minutes silence)

And I am now going to ask additional questions that have come up during this exploration. I'll send out each question as a thought, and then listen to the answer in the form of returning thoughts, impressions, or visualizations.

(3 or more minutes of silence)

All right, it is time to let go of this and return to the present on the count of three. I'll remain in a relaxed, altered state of consciousness, but on the count of three I'll be back in the present time in my current life. And I'll remember every detail of this past-life exploration. But now, on the count of three, I'll be back in the present, remaining with my eyes closed and relaxed and at ease. Number one, number two, number three.

. . . And I am now back in the present, and before awakening I will take a moment to remember what I just experienced and ask my Higher Mind if any of the people in the past life are playing roles in my present life.

(1½ to 3 minutes silence, then read the Awakening provided at the end of the Induction)

Script Two

Teotihuacan/Xocoma Time of Conflict
Past-Life Regression

(Induction first)

In the memory banks of my subconscious mind there is a memory of everything that has ever happened to me in this life I am now living, or in any of my past lives. Every thought, every spoken word, every action from every lifetime I have ever lived is recorded in these memory banks. And I am now going to draw forgotten awarenesses to the surface. In so doing I will better understand that which influences, restricts, or motivates me in the present.

And in this session I am going to explore a lifetime in the city now called Teotihuacan and once called Xocoma. If I were part of it, I desire to explore the time of conflict in A.D. 580 and 581. I am seeking specific information that will help me to expand my awareness of all that transpired in this important lifetime.

So to begin, it is time to step into a tunnel to my own past. I now create a vivid mental impression of a tunnel, and as I count backward from five to one, I will imagine myself moving through the tunnel into my own past. On the count of one I will see myself in an important or clarifying situation that took place during the time of conflict in the Xocoman lifetime.

All right, I'm stepping into the tunnel . . . letting go and beginning to move back in time. Number five, I'm moving through time. I feel myself letting go of the present and moving back into my mental memories. Moving through the tunnel, and way down at the end I see a light. I'm moving toward the light, and on the count of one I'll be there. On the count of one I'll step out of the end of the tunnel and into the light . . . and I'll perceive myself back in Teotihuacan . . . back in Xocoma. Number four, I'm moving through time, allowing it to happen. I feel it happening. I'm moving back in time and picking up speed. Moving toward the light at the end of the tunnel. Number three, I actually feel the sensation of speed as I rapidly move back in time. Moving closer and closer and closer to the light at the end of the tunnel. Number two, I'm getting very close now. I'm almost there. Allow it to happen. Feel it happening. On the next count I'll feel or sense or see myself in an important or clarifying situation that transpired during this lifetime. Number one, I am now there. Allow the impressions to begin to form.

(1½ to 3 minutes silence for past-life impressions)

All right, it's time to move on and explore more about my civilization and my experience. It is a time of the ruler's death. I now perceive impressions about the announcements and reactions to his death. What do I feel about it? What do others feel? The impressions begin to come in now.

(1½ to 3 minutes silence)

All right, let go of this and allow impressions relating to the priests and religious rituals to come into my mind. Perceive anything relating to announcements of the Lord's death and the transition of power. The impressions are coming in now.

(1½ to 3 minutes silence)

And I will remember everything I am perceiving, but it's time to let go of this and perceive impressions of my Xocoman awareness of crystals and power amplified through crystals. The impressions begin to come in now.

(1½ to 3 minutes silence)

And now, let go of this and perceive impressions of flying ships and people from other planetary systems, if they were part of my Xocoman experience. The impressions are coming in.

(1½ to 3 minutes silence)

All right, it is time to perceive anything I can about the conflicts between the priests and the new Lord of Xocoma, the military buildup or fears of the people.

(1½ to 3 minutes silence)

All right, let these impressions fade away, and perceive impressions about the return of human sacrifice, if this relates in any way to my Xocoman experience. The impressions are coming in now.

(1½ to 3 minutes silence)

And I am now going to ask additional questions that have come up during this exploration. I'll send out each question as a thought, and then listen to the answer in the form of returning thoughts, visualizations or impressions.

(3 or more minutes of silence)

All right, it is time to let go of this and return to the present on the count of three. I'll remain in a relaxed, altered state of consciousness, but on the count of three I'll be back in the present time in my current life, remembering everything I just experienced. On the count of three I'll be back in the present, remaining with my eyes closed and relaxed and at ease. Number one, number two, number three.

. . . And I am now back in the present, and before awakening I will take a moment to remember what I just experienced and ask my Higher Mind if any of the people in the past life are playing roles in my present life.

(1½ to 3 minutes silence, then read the Awakening provided at the end of the Induction)

Script Three

Teotihuacan/Xocoma Final Confrontation
Past-Life Regression

(Induction first)

In the memory banks of my subconscious mind there is a memory of everything that has ever happened to me in this life I am now living, or in any of my past lives. Every thought, every spoken word, every action from every lifetime I have ever lived is recorded in these memory banks. And I am now going to draw forgotten awarenesses to the surface. In so doing I will better understand that which influences, restricts, or motivates me in the present.

And now I am going to explore my Xocoman lifetime during the final confrontation between the Xocoman council and the Lord of Xocoma. This was in the spring of A.D. 581, when metaphysical knowledge was hidden by the priests. A new, dark priesthood was created and human sacrifice was reinstated as a religious practice to appease fearful gods.

So to begin, it is time to step into a tunnel to my own past. I now create a vivid mental impression of a tunnel, and as I count backward from five to one, I will imagine myself moving through the tunnel into my own past. On the count of one I will see myself in an important or clarifying situation that took place during this time of conflict.

All right, I'm stepping into the tunnel . . . letting go and beginning to move back in time. Number five, I'm moving through time. I feel myself letting go of the present and moving back into my mental memories. Moving through the tunnel, and way down at the end I see a light. I'm moving toward the light, and on the count of one I'll be there. On the count of one I'll step out of the end of the tunnel and into the light . . . and I'll perceive myself back in Teotihuacan . . . back in Xocoma. Number four, I'm moving through time, allowing it to happen. I feel it happening. I'm moving back in time and picking up speed. Moving toward the light at the end of the tunnel. Number three, I actually feel the sensation of speed as I rapidly move back in time. Moving closer and closer and closer to the light at the end of the tunnel. Number two, I'm getting very close now. I'm almost there. Allow it to happen. Feel it happening. On the next count I'll feel or sense or see myself in an important or clarifying situation that transpired during the time of conflict in Xocoma. Number one, I am now there. Allow the impressions to begin to form.

(1½ to 3 minutes silence for past-life impressions)

All right, I will remember everything I am experiencing, but I'll let go of this and open to perceive more impressions of the fearful things that are happening in the city at this time. What is my reaction? What is the reaction of those close to me?

(1½ to 3 minutes silence)

And I now let go of this and perceive impressions of what is being communicated to me by the temple priests. Is there fear among my people? Let the impressions come in now.

(1½ to 3 minutes silence)

All right, it's time to perceive new thoughts, feelings, or visualizations about the announcement that the Xocoman council will deliver a message to the people at noon on the Lord's Way at the Mu Pyramid. Let the impressions flow into my mind now.

(1½ to 3 minutes silence)

When I heard of the announcement, what was my reaction? Did I decide to join the 25,000 on the Lord's Way to hear the priests deliver their message? If so, allow my memories of this event to come in now.

(1½ to 3 minutes silence)

All right, breathe deeply. Be relaxed and at ease and breathe deeply. *(30 seconds silence)* I am now relaxed and at ease and can put this situation into a multilife perspective. But now, in a relaxed state of mind, I want to ask additional questions that have come up during this exploration. I'll send out each question as a thought, and then listen to the answer in the form of returning thoughts, visualizations, or impressions.

(3 or more minutes of silence)

All right, it is time to let go of this and return to the present on the count of three. I'll remain in a relaxed, altered state of consciousness, but on the count of three I'll be back in the present time in my current life. And I'll remember every detail of this past-life exploration. But now, on the count of three, I'll be back in the present, remaining with my eyes closed and relaxed and at ease. Number one, number two, number three.

. . . And I am now back in the present, and before awakening I will take a moment to remember what I just experienced and ask my Higher Mind if any of the people in the past life are playing roles in my present life.

(1½ to 3 minutes silence, then read the Awakening provided at the end of the Induction)

Script Four

My Present Life Purpose As It Relates to
Teotihuacan/Xocoma Higher-Self Session

(Induction first)
In the memory banks of my subconscious mind there is a memory of everything that has ever happened to me in this life I am now living, or in any of my past lives. Every thought, every spoken word, every action from every lifetime I have ever lived is recorded in these memory banks. And on a Higher Self level I am also aware of my dharmic directions and soul goals as they relate to my purpose in this life.

I know that I was part of the 25,000 in Teotihuacan/Xocoma who made a pact to return every seven hundred years to share the beliefs I love and accept today. Some of us will simply share these ideas with friends or small groups. Others will integrate the ideas into their work or public communications. Some will even devote their lives to this work.

So now I'm going to explore my destiny from a Higher Self level of awareness. I'm already in a deep, altered state of consciousness, and I am going to count myself deeper by ascending into my Higher Self. I will imagine myself ascending into this all-knowing level of mind as I count up from one to seven. Number one: letting go and beginning to ascend, higher, and higher and higher, ascending, ascending, ascending. Number two: letting go now, higher and higher and higher, ascending, ascending, ascending. Number three: higher and higher and higher, ascending, ascending, ascending. Number four: higher and higher and higher, ascending, ascending, ascending. Number five: higher and higher and higher, ascending, ascending, ascending. Number six: almost there now, higher and higher and higher, transcending, transcending, transcending. Number seven, I am now there. And although I may feel little difference, I have at my mental fingertips an awareness of my totality, my past, my present, and my purpose.

And I now call out to my guides and Masters to be with me and to assist me in my quest for greater awareness. Please join me now as I seek an understanding of my purpose.

And I will begin my exploration of purpose by perceiving my dharmic direction. I contend that it is my purpose to explore one of the following directions in combination with a particular soul goal. The seven basic dharmic directions are WORKFORCE, and this includes the majority of general occupations, as well as homemakers.

Two is MILITARY, and includes soldiers, police, and militia.

Three is SERVICE, and includes most religious workers as well as those in medical professions, social services, and welfare.

Four is CREATIVITY, and includes artists, writers, poets, musicians, actors, and entertainers.

Five is SCIENCE, and includes medical researchers, scientists, and space technologists.

Six is PHILOSOPHY, and includes all who present theories about why man does what he does and how to end suffering.

Seven is GOVERNMENT, and includes anyone elected to office.

Now open to higher awareness and perceive my dharmic direction in vivid detail. I may or may not already be following this direction, but regardless of my present path, it is time to perceive this awareness. Which is my predestined direction: workforce, military, service, creativity, science, philosophy, or government? Perceive this direction and everything of importance in regard to this direction. Let the awareness come in now.

(1½ to 3 minutes silence)

And I am now aware of my dharmic career direction, and I open to perceive awareness of the soul goal I chose to explore in combination with this direction. I may have more than one soul goal, but one will be most important, the next secondary in importance, and so on.

The first goal is TO ATTAIN KNOWLEDGE. This means a particular area of knowledge which, when attained on a soul level, becomes wisdom. For example, the desire for direct knowledge of a trait, such as humility, devotion, persistence, sacrifice, selflessness, or perseverence.

The second goal is TO OPEN SPIRITUALLY. This means the integration of spiritual awareness into my dharmic direction.

The third goal is TO ACHIEVE INNER HARMONY. This means to be involved with my life and the fulfillment of my dharma while at the same time attaining balance and peace of mind.

The fourth goal is TO ATTAIN FAME OR POWER. Both fame and power are karmic rewards and offer unique opportunities to communicate awareness and exert leadership.

The fifth goal is TO LEARN ACCEPTANCE, which can be summarized as an awareness of "what is, is." It is my resistance to what is that causes my suffering.

The sixth goal is TO PROVIDE SUPPORT. This could amount to the encouragement and support of another individual in the accomplishment of a jointly shared dharmic direction, or support of a religious or philosophic belief or other cause.

The seventh goal is TO DEVELOP A TALENT. Talents are developed over many lifetimes, so the goal could be in the beginning, intermediary, or advanced stage of creative pursuit.

And again I open to higher awareness and I am ready to perceive my primary soul goal in vivid detail. I may or may not be already working on the development of this goal, but regardless of my present path, it is time to attain this understanding. What is my primary soul goal: to attain knowledge, to open spiritually, to achieve inner harmony, to attain fame or power, to learn acceptance, to provide support, or to develop a talent? Perceive the soul goal and everything of importance in regard to this direction. Let the awareness come in now.

(1½ to 3 minutes silence)

All right, and I now combine this understanding of my dharmic direction and my soul goal with my Higher Self level of awareness to fully comprehend my purpose in life. I trust myself as I've never trusted before, and the impressions are coming in now.

(3 or more minutes of silence to perceive awareness

and ask your own questions. Read the Awakening provided at the end of the Induction.)

Script Five

Teotihuacan/Xocoma Lifetime Dream
Programming

(Induction first)

And I am now relaxed and at ease and centered upon achieving my goals. I am at peace and feel in balance and in harmony. A quietness of spirit permeates my body and mind, and I am open and receptive to positive suggestions. I'll begin with positive suggestions that will be communicated to every level of my body and mind. I am open to these suggestions, which I will accept and act upon. *(Read slowly, allowing time between each sentence.)*

I have the power and ability to program my dreams. Tonight I will dream about my lifetime in Teotihuacan/Xocoma. I will remember my dreams upon awakening. I will remember my dreams literally rather than symbolically and will commit them to paper upon awakening. I remember my dreams, I remember my dreams, I remember my dreams. I dream about my past life in Teotihuacan/Xocoma. My dreams will help me to better understand my purpose in this life. And these suggestions have been communicated to every level of my body and mind . . . and so it is.

That's right. I now begin to dream about my Teotihuacan/Xocoman incarnation, and I remember my dreams upon awakening.

It is now time to use a repeat technique to communicate and saturate my subconscious mind with a message. I will say the words along with myself, over and over:

"I now begin to dream about my Teotihuacan/ Xocoman lifetime, and I remember these dreams upon awakening." *(Repeat 10 times)*

That's right. I do now begin to dream about my Teotihuacan/Xocoman lifetime, and I remember these dreams upon awakening and quickly write them down.

And I am now going to give myself some key, trigger words for post-programming conditioned response. Whenever I desire to dream about my Teotihuacan/ Xocoman incarnation, before going to sleep I will close my eyes, breathe deeply and say these words quietly to myself: "past-life dreams." The words "past-life dreams" are a conditioned-response key to my subconscious mind. When I say these words, I will draw upon the unlimited power of my subconscious mind to support me in the fulfillment of my desires. When I say these key trigger words upon retiring, I will dream of my Teotihuacan/Xocoman past life and I will remember the dreams upon awakening. The words "past-life dreams" now become my key for totally effective conditioned response. And every time I hear this suggestion and every time I use my "past-life dreams" programming, it will become more effective.

And now, before awakening, it's time to use positive visualization and see myself having already accomplished my goal of receiving Teotihuacan/Xocoman past-life dreams. I'll create a fantasy in which I perceive myself awakening, excited about the vivid dreams. I'll see myself writing them down and relating the experience to others. I'll make this mental movie real, and in so doing I communicate my desire to my subconscious mind, which always assists me by generating circumstances to create my programmed reality.

(1½ to 3 minutes silence, then read the Awakening provided at the end of the Induction)

Programming sessions gain power through repetition. Do this session at least once a day for two weeks to set it in motion. Then continue to do the complete session a couple of times a week for as long as you seek Xocoman awareness through your dreams.

Script Six

Teotihuacan/Xocoma Scan-Line Technique
Telepathic Psychic Programming

And I am now relaxed and at ease and centered upon achieving my goals. I am at peace and feel in balance and in harmony. A quietness of spirit permeates my body and mind, and my subconscious mind is open and receptive to positive suggestions, which I will accept and act upon. *(Speak the suggestions slowly, with a pause between each one.)*

I can psychically read the thoughts of others. I trust myself and my telepathic abilities. Every day I become more psychic. I trust the intuitive process. My thoughts have psychic validity and I trust them. The power of the scan line is mine. I use my psychic ability only for the greater good. The words "scan line" are my key words for conditioned response. And these suggestions have been communicated to every level of my body and mind . . . and so it is.

And it's time to use positive visualization and see myself as having already accomplished my goal. I will imagine myself in a vivid mental movie in which I have successfully used the scan-line technique to read the mind of another person. I imagine myself momentarily closing my eyes, taking a deep breath and saying the words "scan line" to myself. I then imagine a line of light shoot out of my third-eye chakra in the center of my forehead and into the mind of the person I'm to read. I then simply trust my own returning thoughts to know the thoughts of the other. I now begin the visualization and experience every detail in my mind. In so doing, I communicate my desires to my subconscious mind, which always assists me by generating circumstances to create my programmed reality.

(2 minutes silence)

And I have just seen my own reality, and I am open to positive suggestions, which I will accept and act upon. I can psychically read the thoughts of others. I trust myself and my telepathic ability. Every day I become more psychic. I trust the intuitive process. My thoughts have psychic validity and I trust them. The power of the scan line is mine. I use my psychic ability only for the greater good. The words "scan line" are my key words for conditioned response. And these suggestions have been communicated to every level of my body and mind, and they have been accepted on every level of my body and mind, and so it is.

And it's now time to use a repeat technique to communicate and saturate my subconscious mind with a message. I will repeat the words over and over, giving them more and more power.

"I have the power and ability to successfully use the scan-line technique of telepathic receiving." *(Repeat 10 times)*

That's right! I do have the power and ability to successfully use the scan-line technique of telepathic receiving. I have programmed this suggestion on every level of my body and mind, and it becomes my reality.

And I am now going to give myself some key, trigger

words for post-programming conditioned response. Any time in my daily life that I want to read the mind of another, I will stop what I'm doing, close my eyes, take a deep breath, say the words "scan line" quietly to myself, and imagine a beam of bright white line shooting out of my third-eye chakra and into the mind of the person I want to read. The words "scan line" are a conditioned response key to my subconscious mind. When I say these words, I will draw upon the unlimited power of my mind to support me in the fulfillment of my desire. When I say these key trigger words I will trust my returning thoughts as the thoughts of the person I'm reading. The words "scan line" now become my key for totally effective conditioned response. And every time I hear this suggestion and every time I use my "scan line" programming it will become more and more effective.

And it's time to create another mental movie in which I perceive myself successfully using the scan-line technique. I now create every detail in my mind —my feelings and reactions—the reactions of others —everything.

(1½ to 3 minutes silence, then read the Awakening provided at the end of the Induction)

It is suggested that in addition to conducting this altered-state session every day, you also work with other people who purposely focus their attention on a particular subject for you to target. Some people will be easier for you to read than others, but everyone has the ability to receive telepathically. And the more you practice, the more psychic you'll become.

ALTERED-STATE TIPS

Body Position

For your altered-state work, try to pick a time when you will not be interrupted and a place where it is quiet. You may either sit in a chair or lie down. If you are sitting, be sure both feet are flat on the floor and place your hands on your legs. If you are lying down, place your arms at your side and do not cross your legs; weight can intensify while you are at an alpha or alpha/theta mental level.

The prone position is best unless it causes you to go to sleep. Avoid altered-state work when you're very tired. Each session conditions your subconscious mind, and you don't want to condition it to fall asleep when you go into an altered state. If you fall asleep twice while in the prone position, conduct any further sessions in a sitting position for a few days.

Your subconscious mind is a memory bank with very little reasoning power; thus it can easily be programmed contrary to your conscious desires, unless you know how to work with it. There is no danger in falling asleep while in an altered state; simply avoid allowing this to become a pattern.

The Environment

Certain conditions are more conducive than others to doing altered-state work. An overly warm room is much better than a cool one. Darkness helps most people to visualize more effectively, so if you don't have a dark room, use one of the sleep masks available in any drugstore. If your environment is noisy, use earplugs. If you're using a tape, use earphones plugged into your tape player. If it is extremely noisy, you may also want to play another tape at the same time to block out the noise. Prerecorded sound-effect tapes of rain or ocean waves are good, and New Age music can also be helpful.

Crystal Enhancement

Quartz crystals are energy enhancers or amplifiers. They seem to add an element of coherence and order to subjective reception. But in all fairness, not everyone can expect crystals to produce a dramatic difference in how they receive while in an altered state. For me, the difference seems to be a subtle variation in clarity, but I know from considerable experience that I receive better when using a crystal. If my wife and I are meditating together, we hold hands with the crystal clasped between our cupped hands.

To use a crystal during an individual altered-state session, hold it in your left hand, palm up, and keep your right palm down. In metaphysics this is called an open circuit. Quartz crystals are composed of silicon dioxide and are formed beneath the earth's surface under high heat and pressure. They are not cut. They have grown exactly as they appear, with six sides and six facets (angles) leading to the termination point.

If pressure is applied to a quartz crystal by squeezing, hitting, or subjecting it to sound waves, the crystal will discharge piezoelectricity. So, even when you are simply talking in the presence of a crystal, there is an energy transformation taking place within the crystal structure. This is an oscillation or vibration that is transformed into subtle sound waves emitted from the quartz.

Since humans are electromagnetic beings, when you talk to the crystal, it sends sounds back to you— sounds that are far too subtle to be consciously heard but that feed into your aura. In addition to spoken sound, today's scientists can measure sonic sound waves that emanate from every part of our bodies. So, just having your crystal close to your physical body causes the crystal to produce corresponding electrical discharges. To put this in scientific perspective, think of early crystal radios. With the help of a coil and speaker, a crystal will audibly reproduce the sound waves that exist in the air.

Crystal experts claim that when you work with a high-quality quartz crystal as a meditation or healing tool, the crystal becomes keyed to your unique energy pattern so that it can focus, amplify, and project your energy. With enough practice and development, maybe it can be used as effectively as Narlo used his in Xocoma.

The strongest energy flow is from the termination point of the crystal through the broadest of the six facets leading to the point. If you want to hold a crystal up to your third eye (brow chakra), place this "window of light" against the center of your forehead. If you tape your crystal to your third eye, place the point up. This technique is ideal when used in an altered state to recall past lives, or for other psychic explorations.

By holding your crystal in your left hand, palm up, and squeezing it slightly, more piezoelectrical energy will be emitted; this, in turn, will flow through your physical and mental body, balancing and energizing your chakra centers.

Remember, crystals are amplifiers—they amplify both positive and negative energies. If you are experiencing negative or unpleasant energy, I suggest you set the crystal aside until you are in a more positive frame of mind.

Retaining Your Altered-State Impressions

Subjective impressions received while in an altered state may fade rapidly when you awaken. For this reason you might want to have a pencil and paper beside you so you can quickly write down the highlights of the session. Or you could speak into a tape recorder so you can keep your eyes closed and verbally commit your experiences to tape while they are still fresh in your mind.

Many people use a second tape recorder (if you're working with a tape), leaving it on while the first tape plays. They then relate their experiences as the impressions unfold. The final result is the same as a past-life regression directed by a hypnotist. Verbalizing your impressions will not bring you out of the altered state; in fact, it's a good way to keep yourself focused on the input, especially if you have a tendency to "trip" or fall asleep.

The Tripping Problem

Once you are conditioned, you may sometimes go into an altered state and not remember anything when you wake up. If you are working with a tape and open your eyes on the count of five, you are not just falling asleep. You may be too good a subject and be "tripping" or drifting in and out. There are several ways to deal with this tendency.

First, try sitting up against a wall or in a chair while in the altered state. You won't be quite as comfortable, but this may help to keep you from tripping.

If you're simply going too deep, don't do any deep breathing before the induction. Once you have become conditioned, you may also want to limit the body relaxation to simply imagining a wave of relaxation moving from your toes to your head. Another technique is to make sure you stay fully conscious during the initial part of the induction by keeping your eyes open until the last seven countdown.

Other techniques that may help if you're falling asleep or tripping out: Niacinamide (vitamin B3) opens up all the deep-level blood vessels within about twenty minutes after you take it. College students often use it to stay fully alert during an exam. I always take about 500 milligrams before going out on stage to conduct a seminar.

A couple of 400 IU capsules of vitamin E and two tablespoons of honey is another upper, especially when combined with a few minutes of strenuous exercise. The honey instantly puts sugar in your system while the vitamin E extends the oxygen. It will keep you wide awake and mentally alert for up to four hours. Don't use this if you've been drinking alcohol, as it will reverse the process, acting as a downer.

Physical Effects

If you feel yourself spinning or swaying while in an altered state, especially toward the end of the induction, don't worry. You're probably trying to leave your body and astrally project. To stop the effect, simply give yourself the strong command "Stabilize!" You are always in control.

A headache that feels like a tight band around the forehead is not unusual in people when they first start to work with an altered state. It is not a matter for concern and will usually disappear within thirty minutes. Some say it results from "third eye" activity, indicating psychic awakening.

Joint Explorations

Touching another person while both of you are in an altered state can sometimes create a psychic connection. As an example, let's assume you'd like to explore the concept of a shared lifetime. Before conducting the session, make the conscious decision with your partner to seek a previous lifetime you may have shared. Communicate this idea clearly to your subconscious minds. Then go into the altered state holding hands. (This will work best if you make a tape of the regression session.) Once the session is over, discuss your results and compare them. To be more objective, write down your experiences before sharing them with each other.

Esoteric Considerations

Some esoterically oriented people feel that they attain superior results with the metaphysical altered-state sessions by following one or more of these occult principles:

- Go into an altered state in a prone position. Align your body in a north/south direction with your head north.
- Remove all metal jewelry.
- Remove all clothing.
- Surround yourself with lighted white candles.

If you've read this far and have explored your past-lives to find out you were part of the Xocoman experience, hello again. If we don't have an opportunity to meet in this incarnation, maybe we'll have another chance to connect in about seven hundred years.

Names & Addresses

Don Tinling
Past-Life Therapist and New Age Counselor
Box 461435
Los Angeles, CA 90046

Alan Vaughan
Psychic & Channler
3223 Madera Ave.
Los Angeles, CA 90039

The Association For Research & Enlightenment
(The Edgar Cayce Organization)
Box 595
Virginia Beach, VA 23451

Secretary of Mexican Tourism
Avenida Presidente Mazaryk 172
Colonia Polanco
Mexico City, D.F. 11587

Hotel Villas Arqueologicas Teotihuacan
Apartado Postal 44
San Juan Edo. Mexico
Telephone 609-09 or 602-44

Dick & Tara Sutphen
Box 38
Malibu, CA 90265

About the Author

DICK SUTPHEN (pronounced Sut-fen) is an author, past-life therapist, and seminar trainer. His best-selling books—*You Were Born Again to Be Together, Past Lives/Future Loves, Unseen Influences, Predestined Love,* and *Finding Your Answers Within*—have become classic metaphysical titles (Pocket Books).

Sutphen is the author of twelve metaphysical books and over four hundred audio and video self-help/self-exploration tapes. He has spent twenty-two years in New Age work and research. Today he conducts his world-famous seminar trainings throughout the country; since 1977 nearly 100,000 people have attended them. Dick also publishes *Master of Life,* a free, quarterly publication that promotes mental, physical, and philosophical self-sufficiency and keeps readers abreast of his latest research and findings.

Dick and his wife Tara live in Malibu, California, where he writes and directs his New Age communications network. To receive a copy of *Master of Life* magazine, please write: Dick Sutphen, Box 38, Malibu, CA 90265.